Women of Appalachia Project

Women Speak

Volume Nine

EDITOR: Kari Gunter-Seymour
LINE EDITOR: Hayley Mitchell Haugen
COVER DESIGN: Kari Gunter-Seymour
COVER ART: Victoria Twomey

INQUIRIES:
Kari Gunter-Seymour, Executive Director
womenofappalachia@gmail.com
www.womenofappalachia.com
FACEBOOK: Women of Appalachia Project

Women Speak

Volume Nine / 15th Anniversary Issue

Edited by Kari Gunter-Seymour

CONTENTS:

Suzanne S. Rancourt

Ridge Runner

bent at the waist she throws her wolf mane to the earth
and backs out of restraints
she'll slip from collar—snap her chain
combust into elongated lopes
streak across Skyworld in greens & fuchsia

fierce in striding stubbornness
no more open heart to those who seek to eat it
no more betrayal or befriending to encase
& capture only to abandon in a cage

exploitation is a blood sport not worthy
of wild beauty where fevers exude
butterflies' yellow blossoms & grass
laid flat by deer or packed down
by short legged bear. Ridge Runner
changes shape on demand
as otter woman she finds silk creekbank slides
slips into seamless water laughing escape
from raven, osprey or any who intend harm
and you're closed out—two chances—that's all you get
that's all you get to comprehend the choices you made
inside windows steam up

if love isn't what you offer
she wolf or otter woman—if
a silent heart is the future—then
let wisdom land as butterflies on milkweed's
fleshy mauve blossoms sticky with lurid scent
turn wrong side out
transform to gold speckled film
emerge
justified

Suzanne S. Rancourt

When the Elephant in the Room Stops Singing

bugle
like bungle, bangle, bauble, beetle (although
somewhat slanted)
babble—language that horns its way
into brass beads, RFID sized rice grains—bugle beads

bugle
played with tongued notes and thin lips
at military funerals, tombs, cemeteries
their blanket rolling sprawl—acres of protruding headstones
unshaved nubs that prickle forth from lawns groomed
and ungroomed—multicolored gramma crocheted afghans
or quilted patrionic squares snapped rigorously billowing waves
shake out life's debris: dog hair, cracker crumbs, potato chips,
earring backs, coins

the bugler doesn't hear them drop
shook free to spatter setting sun's weighted fabric
and bellows comfort, Behold!
another rectangular white stone
name, DOB, DOD, chiseled grief
headstone decals adorn vehicle rear windows
from large to small
so far, our reaching out to be free
our souls exalting false repent
so far, is a bone of stereotypical contention

and the caissons
and the caissons

Randi Ward

Squirrels

Blessed be
the squirrels
that die in a blur
of light licking
salt off
asphalt.

Randi Ward

Grandma

I wind her wrist
watch despite
how she cries
for me to stop
telling time.

Kari Gunter-Seymour

Our Grandmother

twisted silver-streaked strands
into a knot, pinned at the tip of her crown,
draped her bird bones in crossback aprons
cut from calico, sewn on a pump pedal Singer,
bought brand new just after the war,

baked flakey scratch biscuits
from White Lily flour, spoonfuls
of lard, a pinch of salt and sass,
danced the flatfoot clog around
an old wringer washer,
employed on Mondays without fail,

wielded a scythe and hoe
good as any man, grew cabbages
big as watermelons,
drew us maps, where we came from,
patchworks of bloodroot, furled fierce
along the face of the Appalachians,

orphaned us, laid out
under a pine branch blanket,
a rough-chiseled stone.
Redbuds wept purple pearls,
the fields so bare they grew voices.

Kari Gunter-Seymour

Revival of the Fittest

I wake wheezing, airways clotted,
two cinder blocks where lungs used to be,
stumble to car, to clinic, to antibiotics and steroids,
tongue ruined for anything but water,
dog-hungry thirst.

Fever dreams knot bed sheets,
spaces between vertebrae throb,
as if infernally Tasered,
bones wrapped in every small grief—
prickly prayers shouted at a surly white Jesus.

Joe Pye weeds vanilla-coat
window screens and an addlepated
squirrel clings a fencepost,
soaks in restorative rays of sun,
his chitty-song naggy.

Sick time is spiteful, cagey,
buttoning its secrets in sky's light/dark,
furnishing flashes of steam-spewing
humidifiers, albuterol puffers,
dribbles of drool on purple pillowcases.

But thick skin be thick
and a woman like me was made
for muck boots, spade and trowel,
accumulations of dried herbs,
seedpods, deviant doodles,
mocha-crusted coffee mugs.

When my dead Granny's voice coos
from who knows what obscure pressure
of atmosphere, rain about to fall,
I wrestle peevish limbs and morning feet,
quash pinked cheeks of fever, smile
at droplets glittering the parched ground.

Kari Gunter-Seymour

Tucking into the Backcountry

I was punch-drunk
before I got a hundred yards
into that hinterland, chuckled
out loud that I was inside
the woods-wide-web,
no cell phone service,
no GPS, no ding or beep
or breaking news alert,
only the low-pitched purr
of a ticklish breeze.

An avalanche of scents
hitchhiked those airways—
the vanilla of sweet grass,
tang of honeysuckle vines,
spice of root beer
from a downed sassafras.
My nose was leading the way,
compass cased and stowed.

I hid my name inside
other names—grape fern,
spleen wort, wild ginger.
gnarly roots of hemlock
and black birch hugged
rock cliffs, same way
a soaring red-tailed clutched
his dinner, black cohosh
and trout lilies smiled upwards,
heads bobbing like nests
of hungry baby birds.

I snuggled among them,
lying back against warm bark,
hat pulled low, listened
to the music—the nasally honk
of a randied tree frog,
cool clicks of creek water,
shush of the pines, having
left the cicadas a few turns back
to discuss worries of the world.

V.C. Myers

The Stone Age

—After the Mid-Atlantic Derecho, June 2012

The trees were the first to feel it,
boughs bent, swirling furious fists
of lush foliage, twirling green leaves
up to reveal silvery underbellies,
the surest sign of brewing rain.
Wind shivered the river and whipped
the pines, whirling them in tight circles,
wringing them like mops in buckets
of rain as thunder roared from within
the earth itself. Lightning sliced
a weeping willow in half, dropping
its sad arms to split the wooden fence
in the front yard, sending splinters
and sparks through spreading shadows.
A freight train of black clouds barreled
across the valley, chewing powerlines,
and cell towers, leaving us cowering
beneath bridges and clinging to floors
in dark houses. Calendar pages torn
without light or air conditioning in
an unrelenting wave of inhuman heat
and human rage over dwindling supplies.
Then, from dusty mountain hollows,
emerged the wise women, leading
their kin down to the river to teach
us the old ways, their wrinkled hands
working out the history written within
their bones, reminding us that we were
once Earth's children: fed with fresh-
caught fish, drinking pure, rushing
water, scrubbing soiled rags clean with
washboards and rough river stones.

V.C. Myers

Lessons in Mining

—Redneck referred to the red bandanas
that West Virginia miners wore around their necks.
—Chuck Keeney, WV Mine Wars Museum

In my Appalachian middle school, the teachers
transformed the classrooms   into a coal mining town.
A sylvan edition   of Stanford's Prison Experiment.
The rich students worked   for The Company,
while us poor kids played   the miner league.
Whether that division of labor   by social class
was preferential treatment   for the privileged   or
a broader lesson for all,   it lent an extra sting
to our respective roles   in the interactive project.
We miners had to crawl   on our hands and knees,
our necks   wrapped   in red bandanas—
                              identifying pennants
of our mining class   and filters for our breath—
into a dark "mine"   of cardboard boxes and blankets,
a ramshackle tunnel   smeared with black coal dust.
The teachers led us out quickly,   before our lungs
and minds were overtaken   by the polluted air
of the makeshift mineshaft.   Then they took us to
The Company Store,   doled out pieces of paper
Scrip,   and sent us forward   to barter for food   with
smug rich kids   wielding power   behind the counter.
The child of a poor, single mother, I was accustomed
to the bitterness   provoked
     by this lesson   in mining.
Choking in the cardboard coal mine   reminded me
of inhaling bleach fumes,   my face pressed against
my mother's clothes   as she hugged me,
my neck   wrapped   in her red hands—
                              her skin raw
from cleaning houses   of the town's elite, wealthy
parents whose children   looked down on me,
from their elevated posts   behind the counter.
The Company Store setup   felt much like waiting
with my mother   at the Welfare office.   The Scrip
like the stamps she was given   to trade for food.
It made me think   miners must be   like my mother,
parents   trading hard labor   in hazardous conditions,
doing whatever the world requires   of them
to keep their children   warm and well fed.

Sara Pisak

The Mine

*—to my ancestors, who worked in the mines
and passed down a carbide mining lamp through the generations.*

Beneath the surface
    the carbide lamp is eclipsed by soot,
        grime thick
            as icing.
  Not the cake icing of perfect portioned roses,
        marking birthdays,
                but thick fondant soot covering
                    anthracite.
  Anthracite salvaged by hands
    young and old, who pick their way
        deeper,
            into dank corridors.
  Closer to hell, below the surface,
        the flame grows brighter,
                as the Holy Spirit's tongues of fire
                    hovering above disciples' heads.
    Echoing languages of the underground United Nations until
        sediment snares their airways,
                choking off the oxygen
                    needed to extinguish next year's candles.
  By the glow of chemical reactions,
        bronchi cave-in from soot
                but the clean, white light makes it easier to
                    disinter with stained fingers,
                        lumps of carbon, which will
                            descend into the fire.
                                Robbed of transfiguration
                                into glistening
                                    allotropes.

38

Kristi Stephens Walker

Cast Iron

We come from good cast iron, Sis.
Strong and sturdy.

Do you remember those Saturday mornings on Point Lick Drive,
when Paw Paw was up early, a melted dollop of bacon grease ready for his
    flour and buttermilk?
How just before the boiling point, the sound of that wooden spoon dragged
    across his skillet?

Or those reunions with the seasoned elders at the little house up Coal Fork?
It was the center of the universe for them, where the stories they told were
    mixed up,
thick and full,
Someone was spooning peanut butter. Someone was measuring cocoa.
Their tales mixed in to a confectioner's dream, and we swallowed them
    eagerly, every one.

Gathering around the table in that tiny kitchen, while fudge and history were
    being made,
those women held secrets the way the unhurried warming of a skillet holds heat.
Cast iron is slow to warm, but once a good heat is achieved,
Lord, does it hold for a long time.

Rebecca Titchner

A Miner's Song

Coal dust lingers in the ground
Even though the buildings have long fallen down
Ghostly towns, ghostly men
Who wander back to the mines again

I played among these specters in the afternoon
In a place without trees
Whispered promise, whispered dreams
Of a life they would never see

Went with my daddy from town to town
Trying to track these old miners down
Signing affidavits with unsteady hands
Take a deep breath and know where you stand
If only to prove this is how you'll die

My daddy's dented mining pail
Was hanging from my neck
In the hot August sun
We were gathering berries,
we were gathering names
to file a government claim

Coal would write his legacy
but his stories and his money all are gone
My blackened sneakers, his blackened lungs
He crawled on his belly, he was paid by the ton

Went with my daddy from town to town
Trying to track these old miners down
Signing affidavits with unsteady hands
Take a deep breath and know where you stand
If only to prove this is how you'll die

Rebecca Titchner

The Factory Song

Word just came 'round another factory closed down
One more to add to the silence
It's happened before, it will happen again
It's just the way life is in these mountains

We've never been rich
Haven't seen that in years
The good times are just good enough
When you're used to OK no one gets carried away
They just settle for less than enough

People come here from miles around
They love the air that we're breathing
Embrace the big timber and the dusty dirt roads
Some even think about staying

Most tell us we're crazy for hangin' around
And moving to someplace better
Why we're still here is anyone's guess
I could lie and say it's the weather

Generations ago they settled these hills
First it was for the logging
When the mines opened up the poorest poured in
Disappeared in the bowels of the mountains

It's been factory work for a century or more
The roots run deep in these towns
It's gritty and humble and sometimes it's cruel
But folks here are real and they're proud

The ghosts of our past are always close by
To remind us of where we have been
Rows of old factories and red running streams
Tell the story of some of our sins

A long time ago my daddy told me
Get schooling and get yourself out
Like so many others I made my way back
It's a paradise lost and a paradise found

We've never been rich
Haven't seen that in years
The good times are just good enough
When you're used to OK no one gets carried away
They just settle for less than enough

Susan Truxell Sauter

Appalachian Song-Pocket

Vernal signals spill out from ephemeral emerald water
thick with cattails stalks stems under overhanging mother-maple,
   and a longed-for evening lands.

Uphill, I crack a window, let in a curtain of spring-chilled air,
lay my head on bed's cool-pillowed-pool,
   and branch out my limbs.

I fall groggy, meet high-bubbled reach
of spring peepers on tonight's airwave.
   Wood frogs duck-quack their erratic current.

My synapses whir and float with
this hill-caught vocal conflabulation.
   Sound-simmer comes round
      to roiling boil—
         down-hush
                coda.
trill. trill-Trills once again swell
in spring-synchronized musical mayhem.
   I sleep in the hip-pocket
      of Appalachian song.

Dana Wildsmith

What Comes From Silence

—*Accept what comes from silence.*—Wendell Berry

It's hunting season again. I'm a vegetarian, but I don't at all object to other people hunting so long as they hunt ethically and legally. Better a deer should die a quick death by bullet or bow and arrow than by slow starvation in their ever-decreasing grazing range. And better the hunter's children should grow up nourished by meat that's not lousy with hormones and antibiotics. However, I do object pretty strongly to myself *being* the natural meat source shot by some over-zealous and under-attentive hunter. That's why I sing my way through my woods during hunting season.

Yesterday afternoon I treated every hapless deer and wild turkey in a hundred-acre swath of woods to the sound of me belting out "Oh, What a Beautiful Morning" while my border collie Jake and I tromped through pines and sweet gums. Between verses I chatted loudly in Jake's direction: "Whaddaya see there, bud? See any hunters? Yep, sure do hope any hunters notice that we are a dog and a person! No deer here, nosiree." Then I'd flip back to "... the corn is as high as an elephants' eye ..." because I'd rather have any hunters perching unseen in trees think I'm a lunatic than think I'm a target.

Jake is used to hearing me sing when we're deep in the woods, but usually not so loudly or self-consciously as yesterday. Usually, I sing because I'm happy; I sing because I'm free from people looking at me and wondering why I'm singing. I cannot not *Yellow Submarine* my way through the aisles of Publix without becoming fodder for our small-town gossip mill, so I make use of any alone time or alone-ish time in my woods to sway with the lovely old hymn "In the Garden." Anne Lamott says singing this hymn is like "waltzing with Jesus," and she's right. Waltzing through Publix, however, is not behavior designed to cement my status as a mostly upstanding member of Barrow County society.

Sometimes I use any space of private time to make sure I can still remember all the verses of "Angel Band" because I want to take those words to my grave like an epitaph, along with the lusciously old-fashioned lyrics to "Flow Gently, Sweet Afton" and the German text to Beethoven's Ninth Symphony.

Singing also happens to be a logical way of segueing out of my morning's indoor world and into the freer air and light of our woods. But I'm talking about *real* singing, singing that fulfills the promise of the words and notes, not the sort of yammering I was doing yesterday. That was just a survival mechanism, and Jake knew it. My song choices and my chatter were directly counter to the wary mood he sensed in me and so he kept turning around to look at me as if he couldn't decide if he should run find someone saner to walk with or run fetch help for his addled companion.

The truth is, Jake would really rather I kept a monastic silence whenever we walk, and generally that's what I like best, too. The deeper I go into our woods or into any woods, the more strongly I feel I should apologize before I make human noises, though singing seems a bit more acceptable to wilderness than talking, and certain types of songs feel more of a piece than others with the green stillness around. It's the more elegant musical forms that strike me as most fitting to dense woods: anything with a waltz tempo is fine, and Latin texts have an ancient humility appropriate to tall oaks and shaded stands of ferns. Oddly, though, I'd swear the trees and rocks sway right along despite themselves with any Carter Family song. It's apparently impossible for anything living to snub a chorus of "Wildwood Flower". Even Jerry Garcia was grateful for every chance to slip away from his Deadhead following and trip to that high lonesome sound.

So, Jake patiently allows me "… the storms are on the ocean; the heavens may cease to be …" while we're walking along our relatively civilized power line right-of-way or down paths we've cleared through the woods, but he trusts I'll lapse into sensible silence as soon as trees outnumber people by a hundred-fold. And I do. I don't even *want* to sing when I'm deepest in woods, though at any other time I would rather sing than eat, and often have. There's something about deep woods that stops my singing by making me want to listen. I guess what I'm listening to is silence.

I don't mean to imply there are no noises in woods, because there are, aplenty. Crows scream obscenities at me and my little dog, too. A widowmaker limb lets go its last tag of connecting bark and crashes to ground, taking two or three neighboring branches with it. A buck snorts and stomps—once, twice—for me to stay away from his harem. Squirrels clatter to the tops of sweet gums to yell at the top of my head, "We don't like you. We don't like you. We don't like you." A helicopter whoop-whoops a slow aerial crawl over the trees, scanning for those marijuana patches I surely must be cultivating in all my spare time. But these are all sounds with a purpose, a purpose mostly inherent to life in the woods, with the possible exception of the helicopter noises. I guess I could even make a case for helicopter flyovers being essential to wilderness since successfully keeping nervous and short-tempered pot growers out of my deep woods certainly adds to the peace I find there.

To call my woods peaceful, though, may be misleading, as I am reminded when I follow Jake's line of sight upward to vultures circling overhead. I think of vultures as avian ambulance-chasers, but Mama had a more generous attitude toward them. There has been a dead pine leaning near the edge of our woods for a while now. It was tall enough and rotted enough to cause us all to glance nervously at it each time we walked past, or to stomp the gas just a little when we drove past. One morning every craggy branch of that dead tree sported a vulture, dozens of them adorning the pine's skeleton like macabre Christmas tree ornaments, making it into what our Georgia poet David Bottoms calls a "vulture tree". And what was Mama's reaction to this Stephen King landscape? "I felt blessed when I walked past," she told me, "like they were watching over me." I thought it much more likely they were hoping for her to keel over dead so she could be their breakfast, but maybe I'm being cynical.

There are, though, at least two good reasons to be glad about the presence of those vultures Jake and I are again watching as we rest for a minute on the topmost point of our hill. The vultures provide me with a pretty exact compass-heading for where a hunter's kill has fallen. Jake and I can avoid that part of the woods and arrive home un-shot. And if the hunter fails to track his injured-but-not-quite-killed prey to where it fell and died, the vultures will make sure the deer's remains are not wasted.

All this talk of dying has pulled John Rutter's "Pie Jesu" into my conscious mind. I transpose the soprano solo to my alto range, and as Jake and make our home, I shiver at the perfect fit of plaintive Latin liturgy to Rutter's haunting musical lines.

Qui tollis pecata mundi dona eis requiem...

All the way down the hill with my dog, I sing of death, in hopes of keeping us both alive.

Melissa Helton

The Math of a Mother-Heart

• Content Warning: suicide, sexual abuse, gas-lighting •

My eldest teenager is in love. It's that first love. The one you never forget. The one that follows you through life like muted windchimes you can go months without hearing but then a particular gust sets them to clamoring and you're stopped in your tracks in a grocery store aisle, two different salad dressings in your hands as it all rushes back.

No matter how that first love goes or how it ends, it is a landmark experience.

She's in love and doing all those firsts. First time to the movies together. First time meeting his family. First time staying late with him on a school night to watch the baseball game to its conclusion. First prom with a glimmery red dress and his matching red bow tie.

I took her and the boy to get her measured for prom dress alterations. My first time driving them around and spending time with him beyond quick conversations in the school parking lot. And then we went to Walmart for snacks and back to our house where he stayed all afternoon, and she walked him out to meet the sheep, throw rocks in the river, and kiss behind the chicken coop.

It was their 6-month anniversary. And it was the 22-year anniversary of the death of my first love.

On that long ago Saturday, I was in the driveway cleaning my car when my mother called and said they had found him in the high school parking lot, dead of suicide. We had been separated for a few years when this happened, but any suicide loss is terrible. The loss of a first love in that way is eviscerating.

I had seen him just a week before in a guitar store, having not seen him for years. We were catching up on big life events. I admitted how angry I was at a family member who had just died by suicide a few weeks before. My first love said he'd never kill himself that way, the violent way my family member had, that he'd go off quietly somewhere and use his car exhaust. We said apologies for how we had mistreated each other when we were together and when the relationship was ending. He hugged me. It felt like closure. No red flags. No alarm bells in my head.

Six days later, the day before he was found, we ran into each other again at a K-Mart. We hadn't seen each other in years and now it was twice in a week. I was with my fiancé, and we were buying underwear and socks for his daughter who was shipping out to basic training. It was awkward and I waved and said hi, chatted a few moments, and abruptly ended the weird exchange. I admit, I blew him off.

That night, or early the next morning, he did exactly what he told me he was going to do.

I stood in my sunny driveway, holding that phone, saying to my mother on the other end "You're joking." There was no way he was dead. "You're joking."

She finally said "Melissa, why would I joke about this?"

And part of me shattered.

And as I sit in an east Kentucky drycleaners 22 years later on the one rickety chair by the door, my kid standing in a long, sparkly red dress before a mirror, the tailor folding over and pinning fabric, her first love standing beside my chair, his arms crossed and watching with a smile, my heart hurts. They are the ages my first love and I were.

They are in the joy of it. They have not yet had a terrible ending. They may avoid a terrible ending altogether. I hope so.

I feel that burning in my sternum I often feel: my mother-heart that is half jealous, half happy, half proud, half scared.

The math of a mother-heart can add up to well over 100%.

My sternum burning. Like when I took her, my younger teen, and their friends to the trampoline park and I watched them all flying through the air, confident the world would catch them, that everything was conspiring together to protect them from injury and to offer them nothing but delight. The world was their ally and not a threat to assess. They controlled their bodies.

Like when I see that by the end of middle school, they are not smoking a pack a day. They are not avoiding obligatory affection to old men who give a side hug as an excuse to grope their breasts. They are not smoking pot every day when they get home from school.

Like when they tell me *no* to a couch snuggle, feeling the safety and security that they do not have to consent or comply with something they do not want done to them.

Like when they are leaving childhood unmolested, unaddicted, unviolated. Like when they are standing in the joyous parts that can be so fleeting and end so tragically while you're washing your car in the driveway and a phone rings.

This is exactly what I wanted for them. It was my goal as a parent. Joy. Safety. A slow childhood. Making their own decisions about their bodies.

It brings me peace and relief that they have these things. And it makes part of me grieve and re-grieve the ways Little Melissa did not have the same experiences.

When my kids come home safe from a friend's house, I have to hold Little Melissa's hand again, 8 years old, sitting at a friend's kitchen table after a slumber party, being told by the friend's mother, "Now, Melissa, you know that didn't happen," as the father, who had ground his genitals all over Little Melissa's ass the night before, stands in the doorway. I have to whisper in Little Melissa's other ear, "She's wrong. You know what happened. What he did was wrong. You didn't imagine it." And when this friend suddenly refuses to play with her at school anymore, I tell Little Melissa the parents are responsible, that they lied to her friend or forbade her from playing. That Little Melissa didn't do anything wrong to lose this friendship. That telling wasn't something that deserved punishment.

When my kids step away from someone they don't want to hug, or reinforce rules of consent for themselves and each other (like at 5 one saying to an adult family member, "She said to stop, so you have to stop tickling her!"), I have to take Little Melissa into my arms and hold her, tell her that her family member pinching at her 9 year old chest and saying, "I can't wait til these get big" was horribly wrong. That when he said, "Don't tell your father. You don't want him to be mad at you, do you?" when he was done with the other things, he was being evil. That it wasn't her fault.

That all the men who would touch her without consent and in ways that echoed these experiences over the rest of childhood, adolescence, adulthood.… That her feelings aren't wrong. That their decisions aren't her fault or responsibility. That it's not her shame to carry. That actually, she doesn't have to forgive anyone, or try to see the silver linings. That the things her brain blocked out and forgot are ok to forget, that she can heal without knowing and reliving them, that the nightmares and repercussions she feels coming out of these empty black holes of her memory aren't a fiction, they aren't her trying to be dramatic or just be negative and unhappy. That she owes no one her body, ever. That she does not have to pretend to like or want things.

She was thoroughly trained by rape culture that people could do whatever they wanted to her body, and she had to shut up and not tell anyone, not ask for help, just quietly deal with being unsafe and the long-term echoes of fear and pain they gave her for their few moments of twisted pleasure. She had to learn to calculate which of the people are humans, and which are monsters … and when the monsters are so good at pretending and trick us into thinking they're humans, we learn to not scream or tell. We learn to not let anyone see how they've mauled us.

People can be landmines. Sometimes you step around them and are ok. Sometimes you step and are blown to bits. The problem isn't where you stepped. The problem is the landmines.

My first love was abused in similar ways. His landmine was a foster mother. Maybe that is one thing that drew us together. We said we gave our "voluntary virginity" to each other. Our trauma echoes spun both of us off into self-damaging behavior. It spun him off into an eventual psychotic break.

I have to say I'm sorry, Little Melissa, Teenager Melissa, Young Adult Melissa, that you went through those things. I'm sorry that you caused so much damage to yourself and others while you were unhealed.

I'm sorry enough to ensure my kids don't go through this, as much as I'm able.

And when I see my kids not going through these things, but rather going through the delight of childhood … teenagers who are still partially children, moving toward adulthood unhurt in these ways, in love and safety …

My mother-heart burns. Every pain they avoid that Little Melissa went through is a victory. And a healing re-examination of a grief.

So on this day of prom dress alterations, when both my kids are safe and enjoying a lazy day off school, it's all up right under my skin. By their ages, what had I been through? What trauma echoes still laid ahead?

And

What beautiful things are rushing into those spaces in the kids' lives created by the absence of those traumas? What beautiful things are growing in an un-poisoned soil? Look at this first love. It is precious, and echoes of sexual abuse will not poison it. Look at those flying children at the trampoline park. They are so full of squealing laughter. Look at them knowing they can say no. Knowing they can ask for help. Knowing they don't have to keep terrible secrets. So much light is filling those spaces. Look, mother-heart.

I'm jealous. Yes. And sad. Angry. And so relieved. And so happy. And honored to be creating a life for them Little Melissa would have dreamed of if she knew such things were possible. In creating it for them, part of Little Melissa gets to have it too, three decades later.

I want to tell her you did not have to suffer these things in order to be a good mother. But you did have to conquer them in order to.

I want to tell her you're doing it, mother-heart.

You're doing a good job.

Dawn Leas

Sin of Being Okay

—A cadralor

1. You drew triangles, circles,
   squiggly lines in margins above
   math problems with purple pen,
   under reading notes. Teachers
   expected answers you couldn't
   find outside the windows past
   the flat playground, horse farms
   and cow pastures, just
   the tip of your imagination.

2. He dreams in tie-dye—
   each bright yellow flowing
   into pink, green, blue, orange.
   He sees *dream you* before *real you*—
   teased hair, Rugby shirt
   three sizes too big. *Real you*
   rarely smiles, worry lines
   setting into forehead. But his voice
   reaches you, unfolds your mouth.

3. How you describe the color of water—
   blueberry, shallow as
   your grandmother's eyes, violet
   like your cousin's middle name,
   blue as a marble skittering
   across terrazzo in mid-summer sun.
   Muted trumpet in a city club.
   Your favorite pair of Levi's decades old.
   A lover's voice saying sorry for the first time.

4. Define sinoky—
   Sin of being okay.
   Collage of photos with faded edges.
   Lying naked in the woods.
   Water-colored sky.
   Gold star for breaking the rules.
   Crying during sex.
   A dream that can be let go.
   A period with hot flashes.
   Underwater sounds of an abandoned ocean.

5. From an early age
   you learned to be small—
   could fit in a Jack-in-the-Box
   at the slightest raised voice,
   even brief eye contact, embarrassing
   hair out of place. Each person
   cranked—one click, two clicks, three.
   The tighter the turn, the tinier
   you became until the pop splintered your life.

Kristine Williams

Broken

again
and I try
to find my footing
on what should not be a slope
or even a gentle incline
but feels like
riding the leading edge
of an avalanche—
tree tops suddenly underfoot,
horizon shifted,
drowning in white,

Mornings the hardest,
light pours in,
all the cracks
in stark relief.

Kristine Williams

Things I Forget

This is the third damn time
I have stopped in the middle of this room
trying to remember what I came for,
but I know as soon as I get to the basement with
a load of dirty laundry I dragged down the hall,
I will remember.

Is this a poem about memory?

No woman needs me to say that the pain of labor just stops,
while the weight of motherhood begins
with the tugging of a tiny mouth rooting, then latching.

I forget the reason I threw my husband's keys in the toilet in 1994,
although you'd think that I would remember that one. Forget
the name of the 5th grade teacher who taught me to love words and
the number of times I drove an hour each way to Lancaster, Ohio
to get Mexican pizza from Pizza Corner when I was 25 and
the number of times I have run the same one-mile route. Forget, too,
the ache of driving away from a daughter in Pittsburgh,
a son on a university campus
and leaving my grandfather in the ground in Ft, Wayne, Indiana.

Yesterday I passed a stranger on Jeff Hill
who wore my first boyfriend's cologne, I had forgotten
the ache when that boy left the door unlocked the day after graduation,
unexpected nakedness and blue sheets not hiding that girl,
the lifeguard at the pool at his apartment complex.

Why can't I forget the number of hours I cried in the basement
until my mother, mouth pursed, said she signed me up for a class,
that I would go every morning?
Her disappointment so clear.

Sharon Shadrick

My Problem to Fix

I'm not a project, my brother said.
After I rescued him from Brushy Mountain Prison
and took him to church.
Found him a job building pallets
that he soon lost.

Why can't you do things right?
I thought but never said.
Instead of love
I gave solutions.
Instead of listening
I dug deeper,
unearthing toxic foundations
no Superfund could rehabilitate.

Sharon Shadrick

Crushed

A spring celebration for the first college graduate in our family—
Magna Cum Laude, even.
Windows down, the honeysuckle in the May air promised
sweet things.
Ahead, flashing lights. Drivers rubber-neckin'.

Yellow tape surrounded a blue Gran Torino.
My father's car.
I slowed to a stop even though
I didn't want to know.

My father had a way of crushing hope
like a beer can.
Managing it even in his death.

Sarah Diamond Burroway

Hike at Fern Valley

Forgive me for wanting that first August
        for keeping the peace instead of speaking
        for hiding secrets of myself, shadowed in plain sight.
When innocence is blamed, who is sorry for masquerading in lies?

Forgive me for believing broken edges could be smoothed
        for seething behind jagged smiles, half-hearted kisses
        for neglecting dreams, dreading nightmares, disbelieving denial.
When fear confines words, presses them silent, who hears the echo of honesty?

Forgive me for not wanting to hurt you
        for concealing my gashes, cuts, raw affliction
        for blinking back tears through blurred vision.
When real is uprooted and air stops moving, who remembers to breathe?

Forgive me for not wanting the noise of emotion
        for snapping this smiling image of you in my mind's eye
        for ignoring your dangers and not knowing better.
When clouds stop moving, who wants coyotes' howls to mask our own cries?

Forgive me for hating upended feelings
        for sidestepping the ending, delaying decision
        for inferring indifference, shrouding the shame
When faith shapeshifts and stagnates, who hides facts in these crags?

Strong legs pull you up the steep pathway through trees and rocks
        boots crush footprints of deer and quail and the quiet between us
        broken by leaves dancing on sunbeams.
When trails swirl like ribbon, who finds a new path, one that won't circle
    back to this trailhead?

Lacy Snapp

Before Canning

I wonder about the first
person to eat an apple, the process
of biting into that unfamiliar fruit,
not knowing exactly how teeth
would tear through the skin
with minimal effort,
slowed down and cushioned
by that softer layer of underflesh.

Was it a stereotypical red,
or green
or one less obvious: Foxwhelp,
Northern Spy, McIntosh?
Was this new ritual started
out of necessity
or curiosity—an all-consuming
hunger, or just a whim
explored while strolling
by the right tree?

If Adam and Eve
were supposed to be
"the first"—was it like any other fruit
they had experienced?
Those epitomes of perfection
from the garden, divine
textures and juices and surprising
colors and flavors beneath
unsuspecting rough exteriors,
or the softest peels ever touched?

And we've heard they ate a bite
or two
but who was the first person
to chomp an apple down
to its core, with only
a stem as evidence?

One taste—
then an inability to stop themselves
until seeds slipped down

the throat.
Biting and biting
towards an unknown nucleus,
were they surprised
to find
those numerous black eyes
looking out from the snack's center,
a cratered spirit's fixed gaze
staring back—
did they hear ancient prayers
whispered
to not be swallowed,
to instead be discarded into those wild
grasses, an earnest
final hope
to one day could grow anew?

I've had a few
bites taken out of me—
or were they casual knife strokes
on a lazy afternoon
by the riverside,
or were they actually perfect
spiral sheddings
of my soul? Strapped onto
the apple peeler of life, clamped to
the kitchen table, I've watched
ring
after ring
twist down to the floor,
and I've gaped at the subterranean
intricacies I've been hiding
underneath,
both buried intentionally
and by accident.

I have to be ginger with the pressure applied
to the peeling blade
and the speed I choose
for carving away. Too much force,
and half of those insides will stay stuck
to the skin, never make it
to the next steps of the slow simmer,
the spices cooked down
before canning.

Lacy Snapp

Permanence

Fiberglass fragments shimmer
in my palm, embedded
like mica flecks into sedimentary
river stones. My father warned me
not to lean on the frame of the raised
garden bed he made me. Instead of wood
that will rot, bow in time with the weight
of rainwater, he cut four strips of siding
he salvaged from his mobile home park.

I didn't listen—I don't remember to
until it's too late, and so yet again
I leaned on that timeless barrier:
a garden wall he said will last forever.

Folding my body, I gripped the panel
as I dug my other hand into wet topsoil,
no need for metal tools. I carved away
just enough to plant my tomato starters,
then the okra, runner beans, and zucchini,
leaning my body weight into the frame
to reach the middle of the 6 by 6 square.

For what do I need such permanence?

What will I do with a garden wall that never
ages? Each season, the smallest bit
erodes away—mica glass shards rising
up until they need a place to go
and my tender skin will do.

I call him, still, when I need an answer,
and he warns that I need to start relying on
myself, he won't be around forever.

But for now, he tells me to run the water
until it's warm, then hot. To wash my hands
and forearms with soap until the fiberglass
dislodges. To remember next time
to balance myself as I plant bottlenecked
squash in the garden's middle—center
my weight, trust my own stance.

Lacy Snapp

Stitched Curtain Songs

Spider stitches a vertical line
into the window linens.
With each passing year,
she writes of my heartaches
staring insomniac at the blue tv-glow—
nothing actually on except
the Playstation's repeating start screen,
now my only lullaby
for sleeping on the couch alone.

Spider writes of me finding
that thrice folded letter
in my grandmother's jewelry box.
She, in the hospital,
plagued by pandemic.
It was from her mother
to her father from 1946,
before their separation—*I love you with all
my heart, but that's all it means,
for you don't care for me. Here's what
you must know. I am going to marry
a boy that loves me as much
as I love you
and I welcome
how much that is. I am afraid if I wait,
something might happen
that you might try to take
Jackie from me,
for when you crave
someone as much as we do,
you just do things you wouldn't do
otherwise.*

I trace her handwriting as it became
more frantic on the page and wonder
if I've craved anything,
ever. If I've even used
the word correctly before.

Patsy Kisner

Let Me Assure You

I am happy
to be bedstraw
and thistle—
those plants you call
weeds.
Watch how they flourish
in the thicket,
opening their wayward
blossoms
whether or not
you deem them
worthy.

Patsy Kisner

After Death

The wind sweeps
the woods, breaks free
the broken branches,

while inside the barn,
a new calf wobbles
to its feet.

At the garden
sugar snaps wait
for me to pick—

each perfect pea
inside the pods
an assurance
I can keep.

Keri Johnson

Inner monologue on an August evening

The cicadas sing,
And I listen.
However, I note:
The voice in my head sounds a lot like yours.
I reckon 'cause it was one of the first I ever heard.

You and mom recount
That my first words were
"I want my daddy"
—straight to it. There weren't no waitin' around;
No, I didn't have the time to catch on, syllable by syllable.
No, I knew what I needed
(I was "found under a cow patty," too).

I guess since then it's warped;
I got your temper, that stays true.
And I got your heart, but even bigger;
I don't think mine will run out of room.

But I still gotta wonder
Whose voice is it,
When I sit in peace
And look at all I've created,
And all that I ain't;
When I pick the banjo, like your daddy did.

Do you hear your father's voice,
Too?

Meagan Lucas

Quilt Club

When Dreama first invited me to her quilting club, I didn't think anything of it. I certainly didn't think about murder. I'm not crafty, but I know plenty of ladies are so it's not like it's weird, and frankly after months in this town with no friends and only boxes to keep me company, I probably would have been happy to talk to someone wearing prison orange. I was leaving the TV on for company during the day. Carrying a paperback with me to Tyler's practices as a shield to hide my growing loneliness, and ignore the empty bench around me. I was hoping that the looming election season would bring door to door canvassers. I didn't care which side they were on. Just being approached by a stranger was so thrilling my palms were sweating, so I wasn't worried about anything other than if I had bad breath, or if I was laughing too hard at her jokes. Dreama and I'd been talking about how I love to bake, and I thought we were just sharing those get to know you type pleasantries, while standing on the sidelines of Bobby and Tyler's football game, and she'd just asked what church we attended, so you know, it felt innocent.

Excited as I was, it took me a couple of weeks to actually get there; things around here were bonkers. Moving is terrible; I'm never packing or unpacking another box. So, between trying to get settled in the house, and trying to figure out where the grocery store and the post office is, it was a minute. But also, I'll admit I was intimidated. Even though he's been away for decades now, this is Darryl's hometown, and not mine. And he kept making comments about how these women were going to be my new best friends, how soon we'd have inside jokes and be planning a girls' getaway to the outlet mall, and I just kept picturing them asking me to leave.

The first time I went, I brought an Ooey-Gooey Butter cake. It's my mother's recipe; her people are from St. Louis. It's kind of a cheater dish 'cause you use a cake mix for the base, but it always turns out perfect and no one can tell. It's nice to bring something in a 9 by 13 pan too, since I didn't know how many of us there would be. Turns out I'm number six which is a goodly count. I could bring a pie sometime.

I don't have any quilting stuff, no fabric or even a needle and thread, but I figured there would be some there, and there was. Melissa had a whole basket of these beautiful little jewel toned scraps, but we didn't even take them out; it just sat on the floor by the door. Natalie was passing around some drinks, Four Roses that time, but I learned it depended on whose job it was to bring the beverages. Dreama's husband makes his granddaddy's shine and it's a treat, but Laura is always trying to lose weight, so she brings those horrible White Claw things, and we all secretly bring flasks in our purse. So, seemed like it was going to be refreshments and gossiping, and I was pleasantly surprised no sewing, until Dreama cleared her throat and pulled out a notebook, and the other women quit talking and turned towards her. Dreama said: "Larry is still in jail, so we'll need to drop off some supplies to Juanita again. She don't want to take them. Just ring the doorbell and run before she can refuse."

Then Melissa piped in, "The McNieces are still at her mama's cause their Go Fund Me hasn't coughed up enough to get them in their own place. I've heard that the boys have clothes and toys, it's Wanda, you know? She's thick like us, and people keep donating itty bitty stuff. So maybe Kari you could help with that?"

"Surely," Kari said. It was the first time I had heard her speak. At my bewildered expression Dreama said: "Kari works at the Goodwill. If we know what we need, she can rescue some good stuff from the donations before they make it to the sorters."

"Screw the man," Kari said. "You know how much those bastards are making on donated clothes. Assholes."

Then Laura mentioned that she saw Kylie Palmer at the Food Lion with a black eye under mountain of concealer, and sighs came from so many directions that I don't know whose they were, but Dreama flipped some pages in the book. "Natalie," she said, looking over the top of her reading glasses.

"Yes, ma'am, I'm on it," Natalie said, and then added, "You know I saw Martie Nix at the flea market on the weekend trying to sell her old clothes. She's already burned through her jewelry and all Clive's tools trying to pay that goddamn panel loan."

Kari coughed loudly and shook her head, and then before I knew it, Dreama had closed the book, stuck it back in her bag, and then everyone had moved on to what those men were building out by the highway, and if it was going to be a Starbucks like everybody hoped or just another Dunkin' Donuts. It seems obvious now what was going on, but I didn't see it; I didn't know what I was getting myself into. Even when I went home, and Darryl asked how it was and what we did, I said "good, and gossip."

"Figures," he said. "See, you ain't got no reason to be scared of them."

The second meeting they roped me into helping scour Eddie Lee's place; his twins brought lice home from school and Ed was entirely in over his head with those two since their mama joined Jesus. It was complicated by the fact that he didn't trust the pharmacist no more and was trying to only use natural stuff, but apple cider vinegar and mayonnaise were getting him nothing but an infestation. So, we put the permethrin in unmarked bottles and told him it was my granny's recipe. The third and fourth meeting were more the same, and since I'd proven myself not squeamish about the lice, Dreama brought me along to help deal with the rats at her neighbor's place. It felt so good to be helpful and to have this connection. I knew I was lonely, but I didn't realize how isolated I'd been. Their high-pitched laughs, and fruity perfumes, and shared recipes felt like cocaine in my blood; sisterhood. And I didn't think nothing of it when Kylie Palmer's boyfriend disappeared to rehab in California, some said it was Maine.

So, it'd been four months or so, and Darryl, Tyler, and I were settling in. Tyler was getting good grades, he had a girlfriend, he didn't feel like the new kid anymore, and I'm sure that's Bobby's doing. He'd been so kind, inviting Tyler to all sorts of events, keeping him from hiding in his room with those stupid video games. And Darryl liked being back home even if it was forced on us thanks to the paper plant shutting down and his mama dying. He reconnected with his brother and his high school friends. I learned to like it here, too. I didn't think I was going to; I'm used to the land being a little flatter, the sky being bigger. I'm still not convinced that one of these tight hollers ain't going to just fold in on itself and eat me. But folks around here have been real friendly since I started going to Quilt Club, and Kevin has been introducing us to folks who can help renovate the house and taking Darryl to all sorts of events.

Kevin is Darryl's little brother. And when we lived in Canton we used to say "good-for-nothing" in front of little, but since moving home Darryl's dropped it, and when I said it, he said, "No matter what, he's our people. You stick with your people." I'm not sure Kevin's changed much, but he started his own business, he's his own boss and Darryl's jealous of that. When Darryl's job disappeared and Mama Hen got sick, it was an easy choice to move home. But then Mama died, and now all we have left is Kevin. I guess I'm of two minds about it. Leopards don't change their spots, but Darryl says I'm too sensitive about Kevin. He thinks I'm taking my frustration about the house out on him. Like the fact that the roof leaks and there's water in the crawl has something to do with Kevin. It does though, doesn't it? Wouldn't he have known that their mama's house was rotting from the inside? Couldn't he have warned us? Maybe he wanted us trapped in this soggy house? It bothers me too, that Darryl spends all his free time with Kevin and keeps inviting him over for dinner. Kevin licks his plate every time and still feels the need to suggest what I should do to make my meals more appetizing. He has seconds of dessert too, but isn't satisfied unless it's a pie. But he also always brings a bottle of something expensive to drink, and he claps Darryl on the back and says "brother," and teases Tyler about girls but brags that his nephew is the best on the team, and both my men just beam.

It was a few months before I told the ladies about him.

I thought I caught a look between Natalie and Kari, but maybe not. It was in Laura's living room, and Dreama put her elbows on her knees; "Tell me more," she said. And I'm embarrassed now that I said some really petty and spiteful things. It's not his fault everything leaks, and we would have chosen to stay in mama's house anyway since it was free, so it's not like anything would have changed if he'd warned us. And it's good that Darryl has a friend. I guess I just have sour grapes.

"What do you know about his business?" Kari asked. And I was embarrassed again, because I barely knew anything. I have a tendency to tune out when Kevin talks, or whenever Darryl was talking about Kevin. He just irritated me so; I couldn't stand listening to Darryl go on and on about the money that Kevin was making and how he was going to pull him into the business, make him an equal partner.

"Solar power is apparently the wave of the future, what with everyone needing more energy and fuel disappearing. And Kevin helps folks find programs to help pay for their panels, cause it's a special technology. So, they invest a little now, and soon they'll be selling energy to the government and making money hand over fist. They can even borrow the money and pay it back later. And there must be some truth to it, cause Kevin's doing really good for himself." And then I did see the look, and the nod that Laura added, in Dreama's direction. And I figured they all thought I was an idiot to be complaining about this man who was gonna help my husband get started in a good business.

Melissa nodded, and passed around the molasses cookies that I'd made, again. And then Dreama said: "You know what we do here right?"

"Quilt," I said, and everyone laughed.

"That's what we tell everyone else," Melissa said.

"But ..." Dreama said.

"We help," I said. I felt all their eyes on me. "When the creek rises and floods a house, we find shelter and supplies for the family. When someone doesn't have enough to eat, we feed them. If they are cold, we find firewood. When somebody needs to dry out, we get them to rehab."

"Sometimes," Natalie interrupted. "If it's a mama with babies, yes. If it's good for nothing wife beater, well that's different."

"We know all about Kevin," Kari said. "We need your help." I was still thinking about what Natalie said about the wife beater. How this town had less crime, fewer addicts, and a more vibrant community than most around here, and I wondered, at what cost?

"Why?" I asked.

"Because if we waited for the men," Dreama said, "We'd be waiting forever."

"No, why me?" I asked. "I don't know anything about that kind of stuff. I made myself pass out pulling a sliver out of my foot one time."

"You're tougher than you think," Dreama said. "You carried a person in your body and you pushed him out. You raised him and you survived him turning three and then thirteen. You've been married to the same man for 20 years, and we all knew your mother-in-law. If you haven't killed anyone yet, don't sell yourself short. And if you have, well then …"

"What do you want me to do?" I said.

"Just keep your mind open," Dreama said.

"And know those freaking panels ain't free. He's saddling the most vulnerable of us with mountains of debt they can't pay back," Kari said. "He gets them a loan against future production, but there isn't enough, or any, so they end up having to pay. And of course, by then they won't take the panels back. Sucking every penny outta folks who don't got any. It's not right."

"It's always something," Dreama said. "They are always pulling something out of us, out of our dirt, our labor. Now they're fooling us into thinking that our sunshine, what little there is of it, has value, and we can make gold out of light."

Laura started laughing. "There ain't barely any sunlight that reaches into the nooks and crannies of these hollers."

"That's why the special panels," I said.

"Lordamercy they've got you fooled, too," Natalie said. "Next they'll be telling us to farm kudzu; you know, it's awful easy to grow."

And, of course, then it made sense, what they were doing, what they wanted me to do, what good I could do, but I went home more confused than I had been in a long time. I didn't have friends like this in Canton. I don't think I ever have, even in elementary school, even with my cousins, and I don't have siblings. I've never felt this coming together, this knitting of lives, this shared history and future.

And then the answer was easy. An epiphany that wasn't a lightbulb illuminating over my head, but a hand picking up a shovel. This was friendship, family, and community, too; to stand with your people, to do what needed to be done. So, I baked a pie, with enough of Dreama's left over rat poison in it to kill a horse, and I brought it to the next Quilt Club meeting. "I have the answer ladies," I said, putting the pie on Natalie's coffee table.

Jane Hicks

Shears
    —for Rita Quillen

A poet wrote of being a china teacup,
a mug, a gravy boat—a description
of her life stages—form related to function.
I think in terms of tools—tiny stork-shaped scissors
to help embroider, show skill, dexterity,
the patience of a lady. All busyness
and motion, I lost those, went straight
to fancy scissors for cutting shapes
of patchwork and mending rents
in garments. I could stand
at the table, move my feet, tap my toes
while I cut. Pumping a treadle machine,
or swinging my feet while running a tight stitch
at the quilt frame gave me patience to control
the fabric to my desired form.

I hide those scissors from forgetful husband
and paper-cutting grandchildren, instead
deploy functional scissors and shears
in tool drawers, junk drawers, and craft boxes.
I sit, watch from this form I've taken as the
clock winds down—my flittering busyness
in my head, not feet.

Jane Hicks

Straight and Narrow

"You'd catch a toenail in a stitch that long,
jerk the covers right off the bed."
My grandfather peered over my shoulder,
patted it, and passed through.
Astounded he would consider our lesson
at the quilt frame, my grandmother
peeped over her glasses and nodded.
I giggled at his assessment but
it gave me a gauge to stitch by,
to rock the needle straighter
and tighter like the rows he plowed
in their vast garden or the way he packed
tight hands of tobacco on a market basket.
I think of him that way—neat and spry.
Even in farmer overalls, he was trim,
straight, and true like the stitches
his words conjure as I apply my needle
to any project or myself to any task.

Jane Hicks

Journal

Sifting through my journal, I found
notes on a fox squirrel, eating rind
of pumpkins put out for deer after life
as Halloween lanterns, a doe coughs,
snorts, squirrel scampers, scurries
up a leafless November mulberry
birds and animals love in late spring.
Deer on the ground, as squirrels fling
from branch to branch, launch
sweet purple berries for the does' lunch,
the foxes' dainty breakfast,
or a plum and lilac gloaming feast.
Yellow, plate-size leaves
affixed until frost cleaves
them, a bold carpet of gold,
becomes favorite meal of does
and their once-spotted fawns that graze
unaware as mothers watch, raise
alarm at sudden motion or scent
of downwind as bucks insistent
upon their hunt for a mate
snort, mark trees with antler scrape.
Darkness rendered my journal
unreadable, but I recovered kernels
of poems and memories of a russet
squirrel on a pumpkin tuffet.

Kathleen Driskell

Mowing the Fairways

One summer, at the local course,
I spent my hot days driving the beat-up
Allis-Chalmers, black smoke burping

from its stack. Up and down
the fairways of the back nine
I rumbled, bush-hogging the rough.

I stopped looking behind me
After the first day, when I realized
I was moving over nests of young.

Once, a shredded snake flew
overhead, strange tentacled bird, thrown
up from the churning rusted blades.

It was how I was going to escape, to get myself
to college, after the sheriff had run away
my father. How I would become a nurse,

Or a teacher, or a paralegal. Something
useful.
            I didn't have to begin ducking balls
until around lunch, when the duffers

who'd told lies to escape their offices
for the afternoon, sped about in carts
for a quick round. Once, cutting

farthest from the clubhouse,
I watched three men
in bright orange jumpsuits

navigate the wood's edge. They saw
that I saw them, but we all pretended
I hadn't. They kept moving.

I kept mowing. Trundling forward,
we were all—I guess—pretending it
didn't matter where we'd just come from.

Kathleen Driskell

On Cleaving

All summer I watched for him. I knew he was out there,
inside the rimming of woods that ran all around.

Wild boy, his feral curls stiff and ashy with dirt,
he pedaled past at least once a day on his rickety rusting

bicycle, grocery bags dangling from crooked handlebars,
his filthy sleeping bag tied to the rear fender. One

neighbor said she saw him washing dishes at the Waffle House,
near the exit ramp. Another called the cops, but no one ever

found out what he was hiding from or why. Though I tried
to stay alert, he always approached quietly, giving me a start

while out front pulling weeds near the picket gate. Each time
he appeared, my heart revved up in faster time, my eyes anxiously

searching for my small children nearby, digging happily
in the dirt with old spoons. All summer, he must have lain

in the woods, awkwardly tending his fugitive camp, trying
to slow his own heart leaping up with each odd bird call

or snap. In the night, I'd wander from window
to window, watching, making sure his flame

had not caught hold of the horizon. I buttressed for
danger, instead of worrying over him like a good mother,

instead of extending him any kindness, if only
in my mind. So many ways my children have cleaved

my heart tenderly toward the world; and so many ways
they've turned my grizzly core against it.

Kathleen Driskell

What the Girl Wore

At the store, on the hanger, the blue dress must have fallen
like water to a froth of frilled hem, its bodice as smocked
as a christening gown. A season out of date, her mother chose it
from our local department store chiefly for the high collar,
but I knew it was a dress Lisa wouldn't have been caught
dead in. Just hidden under the neckband of lace the circle
of her purple necklace, each dark bead a fingertip of efficient
bruise that we already knew about anyway, and simply went on
imagining, as we, her classmates, filed past the white coffin.

KB Ballentine

Keening

No sense of season or hour, the cairn's top rock
    disappears in a swirl of mist then the whole of it
      cloaked completely. Everything the color of milk,
    dull—sight, sound, taste all dampened at the summit
of this mountain. Life after you.
    No fissure in this cocoon of nothingness, only fear
      of the unknown. Below the alpine line the view is clear—
contours of each notch, each gorge, each furrow and fold
where stone heaved then settled—its place secure,
    permanent. All done before us. Without us.
    But this cairn, formed by piling broken stone on stone,
    inhabits only this moment. Marker to one, omen to another:
waypoint to somewhere else. It is the key that releases
    this fist in my chest. I seize the emptiness, reap nothing
                         —offer my cries.

KB Ballentine

Digest the Dead

Coyotes howl through a rising snow moon,
deer—heads up, twitch tails and listen.
Is it tougher to see in the dusk
        or is it just me?

Life changes without notice—
one February much like another
        until it isn't.
Untroubled, the deer move off,
but I wait on the ledge, watch clouds
pebble the sky,
            river a dark coil below.

The moon's cold glare crests the ridge,
        tracks the jagged scratching
      of a ghost
roaming these woods, hearing the growls—
  believing there's still time.

Your absence gnawed
        my heart to nothing.
The cut was quick but not clean.
What scraps of memories left
      were devoured in shadows—questions
of a life worried to the marrow,
        a hollow bone unfleshed.

KB Ballentine

The Darkening

Say you stayed, say you learned
   the courage of red birch leaves,
to cling through winter storms,
   other trees only stark branches
holding snow.

Say you persisted, say like rain
   you found a stone and focused
your gentle and driving drops
   until crags resolved into puddles,
into smoothness.

As we breathe, the universe unspins,
   reds and golds like a phoenix spiraling.
The darkness of galaxies sing themselves
   past silence like mice, a song too piercing
to bear.

Say you had believed, that as each star
   finishes long before its light, your love
echoed through my skin, and your story
   will go on, though you didn't stay.
Though you couldn't.

Rose M. Smith

Eight Inches at Morning

Great snow for igloos comes to mind,
then *if the kids weren't states away*
and *not about to sit in a small block house.*
I push another shovel load across
the black divide, my back screaming a long note
here instead of singing.

Each few minutes, pause, scan, notice:
No young entrepreneur anywhere in sight.
Inwardly, I lament how much we've changed
in this century newly grown. Then
Bill from down the street intros himself,
two shovels in hand.

We meet mid-way, tackle
the driveway's full back half
over stories of the halfway house
down the street, right next to his,
and the young man who'd better never look
sideways at his daughter again,

of the son he texts he misses on days like today,
and how Bill also thinks he's too old for this.
We tackle the mountains up front left for me
by an over-zealous plow, consider them great
argument for condo life, and almost
wish I had not shaken off that one guy

who told me online he was six feet tall,
loved poetry nearly but not quite right
before warm Spring. He'd worked so hard,
put on a pleasant face, asked far too soon
where I thought *we* were going.
It was not about the height. It was the lie.

Bill and I shake neighbor hands when he goes.
Later, two doe near the fence flick their ears
just enough to draw my eye, remind me they
tolerate that six-point buck only when they wish.
When something in Alone can't satisfy
what the Something With can offer.

Rose M. Smith

First Bike

They say Willie was a fine young man
the one time we had nerve enough to ask,
but by the time we filled Virginia's house again
with bare feet, hungry, nappy heads, knobby knees,
he had already ridden his runaway bike down the slope
to hidden memories seldom rattled, stirred, mentioned.

She slipped one evening and Willie peered out
at us, between rare tales of favorite trees, suitors
who came calling on fathers before a girl agreed,
and dirt-blowers—we tried to imagine them, men so short
they'd send up clods of Alabama dust with each exhale.

A fine young man, that seventh son who had been first.
We did not know we weren't the first who'd longed to
follow in his tracks—around the stone driveway,
up the sidewalk and down, out
into the silver flash of a daydreaming trucker's
stunned and disappearing smile.

We felt his fender scrape the legs we stood on,
chill kiss of curbside against our falling heads.
We watched the wheels of our requests
spinning on their sides.

We fell asleep to the blast of horns,
Willie James' missing face fighting for light and shape,
Virginia's blood riding on the curb
but never in the street.

Pauletta Hansel

For the Friend Who Asked Me to Write a Poem About Breonna Taylor, 9/23/2020

Because she said today the only words
she had to say were ugly.
Because injustice is a dark shot
that always hits its mark.
Because a knee on the neck
of a dying man
has lost all metaphorical possibility.
Because a sleeping woman cannot say,
"They'll kill me. They'll kill me."
Because they did.
Because they will again.
Because I live with the luxury of breath
I give this breath to say their names
more beautiful than any words of mine:
Natasha
Janisha
Meagan
Maya
Sandra
India
Betty
Korryn,
Deborah
Charleena
Atatiana
Breonna

Pauletta Hansel

Com/passion

Loaned across the languages,
to Latin   from Greek to
    com "I am with you" and
    passio, "I suffer,"
of the kind that is kin
to adoration and Christ
on a cross and suffer little children
to come unto…   *Pati,* the same root
    as in patience and
        patients,

the acronym, PATI:
    Penetrating Abdominal Trauma Index;
        Public Access to Information—
too much information
leads to compassion fatigue.
    "The near enemy"
of compassion is sorrow, is pity, is
    handwringing,
        ass sitting,
            woe unto-ing
every last one of us:

    the "pathological empathy of our age"
is compatible with Twitter
and Facebook and "idiot compassion,"
the general tendency to give people what they…
    ♪ … can't always get …♪
because you can't stand with their suffering
long enough
    to be what they need.

What you need.

What I need…

    "A heart
    broken open
    like a geode to the rare space within,"
says *Roshi* Joan Halifax.

I am with you, buddy,

       (*Buddy*: mid-19th century; perhaps an alteration of rother, as in
       "can you spare … ?")

my heart on permanent loan.

Pauletta Hansel

Dis/traction

Drawn asunder,   dragged,
as
          by tractor,

"a poor mad soul," so driven   /   or split,
          as in
                    "I was
                              of three
                                   minds, like a tree in which"

                                   there's an iPhone,
                         a book, and down below, my
               body, rooted still in good
dirt.

Karen Spears Zacharias

The Divorcee

An ambulance pulled up to the curb. A team of emergency responders, wearing navy slacks and matching jackets, exited the back end of the yellow-and-white vehicle. Kneeling beside a woman who had fallen minutes prior, they began to administer aid. I couldn't tell if she tripped or if she'd had a stroke or if someone had run into her. That would be for the team of specialists to decide. I stood aside, pressing my back up against the window of advertisements in the Poundland store.

One of the men scanned the gathering crowd to see if anyone knew the woman. No one stepped forward to claim her. One of the medical teams held a compress to a cut over the fallen woman's ear. Blood seeped out and puddled on the sidewalk. Her shoulder bag had fallen along with her and its contents were strewn out into the street. The youngest fellow of the medical team picked up the woman's cell phone. The locked screen provided him with no information.

"Her name is Sonja Saad," I offered.

"N' who er ye?" the young man asked. "Er ye related?"

"No," I said, shaking my head. Sonja was being lifted into the back of the ambulance when one of her shoes fell off. I picked it up and handed it to the young EMT. The crowd began to disperse, off to complete their shopping and errands on this Friday. It was those red heels of Sonja's that I had noticed when she first walked into the boutique clothing store. I have a soft spot for expensive Italian leather.

"Love your shoes," I said, as she weaved around me.

"Ah, thank you," Sonja replied.

"Boston?" I asked, noting her accent.

"Burlington," she said.

"Oh! My husband and I made our first trip there last summer. It's a lovely place."

"Did you?" she said. She placed the gold chain necklace she'd tried on back on the counter.

"Yes. We have friends who live there. Bob and Lynn. They moved there a few years ago from North Carolina. They love it there and now so do we."

"I left there in 2013," she said.

"To come to Scotland?"

"In a roundabout way," she replied.

"I'm Karen," I said. "I'm from Oregon."

"Sonja Saad," she replied. Neither of us shook hands or removed our masks, keenly aware of the protocol for protecting one another's health in such a small space. The orange jacket in the window had drawn me in. The price tag on it had quickly dissuaded me of any temptation to try it on.

"Oh, look at this," Sonja said, picking up a Powder brand scarf. "These rabbits are adorable." She referenced the fabric's print design.

"They are," I said. "I love the whimsy of this brand. I don't think we have this brand in Oregon."

"Perhaps not," Sonja said. "I never knew of it until I came to the UK." As she draped the scarf over her shoulder, I noticed a tattoo on her wrist: *Rising on the other side.* It followed a line that drifted into three mountain peaks. Sonja noticed me reading her tattoo. "I got it after my divorce."

I nodded in recognition. "You don't have to explain," I said. "I didn't mean to pry."

"No worry. Lots of people ask me about it." Sonja tucked a loose strand of dark hair back behind her ear. She wore gold loop earrings and matching gold bangles. I guessed her to be in her mid-40s; although, with cosmetic enhancements, she may be in her mid-50s. So hard to tell anymore. "You married?"

"Yes," I said. "Going on our 44th this year."

"I can't even imagine," she said. "Hey, you hungry? There's a teashop next door. Would you join me?"

I was taken aback by the invitation. Since arriving in Scotland, most of my time had been spent seeking out adventures on my own. I don't mind hanging solo, but I'm unaccustomed to not being sought out for social engagements. I missed conversations where people took an interest in me. I was delighted to be included.

The tearoom was even smaller than the clothing store. There were four tables set with linens and fine dinnerware. The vanilla candles and white lights made it a welcoming place. Fortunately, we were the only guests. The host sat us in a corner and took our order for scones and spice black tea. Sonja's phone buzzed. She glanced at it and then dropped it into her bag.

"So, what brought you to Troon?"

"Nothing in particular," I said. "Someone on the train told me it was a nice beach town that I should check out."

"And?" Sonja spread out her palms as if expecting to receive something from me.

"It is a nice beach town. Charming shops and I love the Ferris wheel on the promenade. Very scenic."

"Have you been to the Fairy Trail yet?" she asked. Sonja removed her mask and placed it in her bag. Her teeth were a brilliant white, and straight. A sign of good dental insurance or money. She had a diamond stud in her nose.

"No. I read about it and do hope to find it on another trip."

"You'll have to let me know when you plan to return, and I'll take you there myself."

"That's very generous of you," I said. "I'd love that. Maybe when my daughter comes to town."

"When is that?"

"May sometime."

The hostess placed pots of tea in front of us. Mine was a light blue. Sonja's was a sunny yellow. Two sugar cubes each, along with a miniature jug of milk. Then she brought over plates of warmed up scones, with butter and strawberry jam.

"We call these biscuits where I'm from," I said, laughing.

"There was this place in Burlington that I used to go to. They made the very best biscuits," Sonja said as she sliced open her scone.

"Do you miss it?"

"Burlington? Sometimes," she said. "I miss the friends and the job I had there. I miss the summers on the lake, but not so much the winters. And I don't miss all the shit I had to put up with."

"Sorry," I said. "Didn't mean to bring up a sore subject."

For the next hour Sonja confided how her marriage of 20 years busted up. A familiar story of infidelity known to women the world over. In Sonja's case it had been particularly painful. She was married to a doctor who left her for another woman, but not just any other woman. Her sister-in-law. A woman Sonja had considered one of her closest friends.

"So your husband not only betrayed you but betrayed his own brother as well?"

Sonja nodded.

"Their family gatherings must be fun," I said.

"He not only had an affair with her, but he also married her after we split up."

"Ohmygod, really?"

She nodded again.

"Your husband divorced you and married his brother's ex?"

"Technically, I divorced him."

"Did people around Burlington know what was going on?"

"Sure," Sonja said. "It's basically a small town. People know each other. He was a doctor and so was his brother. Pretty hard to hide that sort of thing."

"Was she pretty?"

"Who?"

"Your sister-in-law?"

"Not really," Sonja said. "But she was compliant, and it's been my experience that men who cheat seek out compliant women. They prefer the kind of woman who never challenges them to think, or act. They are willing to let men be as jack-assery as they like."

"Jack-assery? That's a new one." I pulled out a notebook I keep handy and wrote it down.

"Can't think of a better way to describe such behavior."

"So why Scotland?" I asked. "Why not Miami or Minnesota?"

"One was too hot, and the other is too cold. Troon's temperature is more moderate. Besides, I had a college roommate who lived here. She urged me to come, and at that point I wanted to get as far away from my ex as possible."

Sonja and I finished our tea. We exchanged phone numbers, and I promised to text her to let her know the next time I'd be in Troon, so that we could take that hike together. She picked up the bill, refusing to let me pay for anything.

"My pleasure," she said, tapping her American Express card. "It's good to have someone from the US to talk to. Even after all these years here, I still can only understand half of what these locals are saying." We both laughed.

"Thanks again," I said. "I hate to run off, but I want to stop by the vegetable market and pick up a few things before heading back to Ayr."

"No worry," she said.

It was the last thing Sonja said to me. I'd paid for my peppers and limes when I heard the ambulance. I stepped out into the sunlight to see Sonja laying there on the street, bleeding, and being attended to by the team.

My inclination was to rush in, to claim her as a friend, to call somebody.

But who?

I didn't know a soul in Troon. And despite having shared the past hour or so with her, I didn't really know Sonja Saad. I hated the thought of her going to the hospital alone. I hate being alone when I am sick or hurt. I want to be lovingly tended to in those situations. It's not right to assume everyone is like me though.

So as the ambulance drove off, I stood back and said a prayer that just has she had been doing since leaving Burlington, Sonja would once more rise from the other side.

I texted her last week to see how she's doing, to see if we could schedule in that hike we talked about.

She hasn't texted me back yet.

Rhonda Pettit

All the Pretty Little Losses

How did you sing them to sleep, Milly?
What had been sung to you?

Was it a hymn, a ballad, a psalm you hauled
with your seeds

from the Piedmont? Did words arrive without
melody? Did you

make one as you made your way through
the days—humming

a tone from birdsong, following the lilt
and fall of a human

voice or the rhythm of ax and wood? Did worry
or weariness stop

your composing, only to echo
forward a chord

you don't remember hearing? Or did a word dis-
appear, letting you fill

the void (what was your word)? Did a lullaby grant
more than sleep:

voice holding notes, hands holding child, all holding
the same song, river

the refrain? Did you believe once sung it was forever
somewhere?

Did you hope that the trees would listen
and remember,

that roots would absorb and be absorbed
and hold?

Did you dare not say this to anyone and instead,
sing?

Is the compass of your voice forever lost, or is it
here?

Barbara Sabol

Holding

The place wavers through dust as I turn down
the long, gravel drive. A rustic mirage. The way
I see it in dreams.

The farmhouse hunches like an old man.
Its white paint peeling from staring too long
into the Appalachian sun. Windows glazed over.
Beams a bit off plumb.

How my family loved this land—seventeen full acres
of field. Some devoted to soy, an ample garden.
(Best stewed tomatoes in Washington County.)
The rest Dad let go to bunch grass and clover.

Summers, grasshopper rasp deep in the lea. Snugged
in the long reeds, I'd watch fireflies set the meadow alight.
The house stood like a beacon amongst all that bounty.

Gathering itself beneath the eaves, the place braces
for a final round of weather. Fog sighs through the rooms.
As I pull away, a sudden gust rustles the windbreak of pines.
I feel its bite in my own old bones.

Jessica Thompson

Cradlesong for a Crone

Standing at the sink, wrist deep
in water, my hands the heart

of this shiplapped room,
remembering my sisters

in the kitchen of our youth—
doing the dishes.

The bubbling laughter,
our lullaby voices.

The bluish whites of our eyes,
our long, unencumbered hair.

A step stool at the sink,
the heavy pots,

the sweeping of the floor.
Shipwreck

when one of us left—
the slamming of a screen door.

This salty water.

Mikelle Hickman-Romine

Wildcrafting

I've been eyeing wild grape vines for months,
envying the long twines of their reaching arms,
hoping for some gratitude as I offered to cut them
for weaving, for a chance to feed my newborn self
nursing the breast of her land mother
now that her flesh mother is ashes

next to my dead mother's filthy trash hoard
(all the scraps of stuffing her maw with a restless dream)
the wild grape is dragging a honeysuckle over the fence
miraculously full of red fruit turning black
blue with bloom and shockingly gamey when
I break a grape in my teeth and spit the pits down

the neighbor, he is generous with his weeds, says
take what you want, don't eat the poke weed fruit, my sister
vouches for me and says if anyone knows the difference
I do
he's going to take a backhoe to it anyway
to save the bulging fence he's going to raze it all to the ground

So with my gloves and my knife I wait until the fruit is black
and the leaves are yellow and I pluck all the fruit I can find
that didn't grow out of the motor oil slick oozing from an old truck
I take five sycamore saplings, too, strip the leaves into a trashy heap
and a tangle of wild vine as big as a body in my arms

The scent is strong and troubling, a green sap scream of protest,
the fruit a soft groan in comparison, the easy sacrifice and
the mother dear, the future and all hope of a future gone in a swipe
of my knife, not drowned in the scent of burning fuel and the
rumble of a steel tread grinding like it will be in a month

No, this is personal work, just a knife and my restless dream,
culling the fruit of the poisoned vine and cooking the rest
to syrup of miraculous purple, using the yeast to make bread,
weaving the doomed land into a new future
nursing myself until I can grow

Mikelle Hickman-Romine

Andy

my father swore he could fix anything with a torch and a hammer,
that small Appalachian wizard, hair snow white from a forty foot fall,

blast it to cherry red then hit it twice,
it was a spell that pushed it from broken to something else

functioning in a frail state of attention and string theory
so he rewired his home with impossible electricity

kept coffee cans full of rusty water and nails,
smoke and motor oil to bind it all down

the old six of seven sons, his mad mother loved him
and shoved him out the front door to fight

so he called me honeypot when I was tiny,
loved me for stealing food off his plate

I was his little Spartan warrior, blessed cherub with pointed teeth,
I stole his musted purple grapes off the vine and sucked their pulp

so we were sweethearts, my grandpa and me,
working class mages smelling of forges and glue

He built my first tools for me, hand made me a cedarwood box
with a roll top lid for my juvenile workings

I have a little of his power
and my hair grows in whiter every day

Karen Paul Holmes

Driving Behind Rose in North Carolina

I follow my friend after the memorial of our mentor.
We pass tarpapered fishing shacks along Brasstown Creek,
where I'd be too prissy to stay but can imagine
fishermen happy as trout.
The backbone of the highest ridges beyond us is still brown—
thinner air hanging onto winter.

But down here, fallow fields bloom yellow.
Rose would know what it is—she who relishes bare feet in soil
and communes naked with the midnight moon.

There's the decayed mill declaring *KEEP OUT,*
then a makeshift *Boiled P'Nuts* stand with its bubbling 55-gallon drum
and the occasional red-dripping *REPENT* nailed to a tree,
which always gives me, though I know better,
the every-hair-on-my-head heebie-jeebies.

In the last ten minutes, I've seen three over-zealous groundhogs,
dead, so I tell the live one on its hind legs in the ditch
don't cross, honey.

Curls of razor wire glint in the jail yard's sun,
and a white-steepled church proclaims:
Cars aren't the only thing recalled by their Maker.
We see fewer Confederate flags these days, thank goodness.
But here are some draped on a rusty truck by the roadside, $10.

Before Rose and I met, friends kept claiming *you'll love each other.*
I know she's recording the valley's life too—
the way our poet-mentor taught us. The way our words outlive us.
Rose and I hug the curves like best friends, a cord from her car pulling mine
past black cows in grazing posture, white faces down,

her listening to Prince, me to Pavarotti—voices rising
from the same marvelous mind that greens
these farms and mountains come spring.

Natalie Kimbell

To the Melody of Rain

The slow rush of rain brings
my grandmother to sit with me
on the porch to break pole beans.
Her shoulders curve as she gathers
herself on a cane-bottomed chair
snapping beans, dropping them
into a metal basin that echoes
the dull cadence of a million steady
droplets hitting the gutters.

The air fresh and warm like garden greens
piles on my lap. I anticipate the snap,
unzip the tip from its smooth knobby pod
down one side then, tear and pull loose
the strip from the other side.

I close my eyes and break
the bean into bite-size pieces.
I listen and try to match Grandma's pace,
but it's only the rain's patter. The air vacant
                                  in my hands.

The flutter of tree swallows stirs me,
each blue-wing streak captures mayflies.
Their lives so short,
and yet, whose life is long enough?

The rain lessens,
leaves puddles to mark the earth
leaving the memory of where it struck. I rub
my palms against the thighs of my denim jeans
and lean in for the last strains of the rain.

Wendy McVicker

Eye/Us

They are like paper
dolls, these girls
from 1961, swinging
arm–in–arm along
a cobbled street—
scissor-sharp bodies
and slicing glances,
their pointed toes aimed
straight at the camera.
The tall one in the middle
tosses her sparkling
hair, and her sisters
lean in close
as to a warming flame.
They prance like models
on a runway, pinched
by narrow skirts
and garter belts
and the old, old need
to be sexy and pure
at the same time.
Please look—but
don't touch—back off,
outside the picture,
neat square marked
in black. Watching,
we know those borders
will crumble soon—
but in 1961,
for these girls laughing
by the canal,
they are unbreached,
dolls not yet torn
from their paper
pages

Cat Pleska

My Mother's Sighs

The cartoons were the thing. Bugs Bunny. Elmer Fudd—Wabbit season! Duck season! Pepe LePew, the skunk, and my favorite. He spoke French. And it just so happened, in Mrs. Grimm's 3rd grade class, another teacher would come in for a half hour and teach us French. So, I understood Pepe perfectly. He was in love all the time. I knew it because he kept saying "*Amour*" and "*Ja'taime!*" which means I love you! And then he sighed, all moony-eyed at the cat with the white tail stripe, who Pepe thought was a skunk. Of course the cat/skunk knew better and vamoosed, away from Pepe. Pepe kept sighing, longing for his love.

Every afternoon, I arrived home from school around 2:45. I dove into my homework and finished it because my mom said if I didn't I couldn't watch *Mr. Cartoon*, which came on at 4:00. That's when she went into the kitchen to cook dinner. My dad, who worked day shift at Kaiser Aluminum, was supposed to be home from work around 5:00. So, during commercials I'd hear her banging pots and pans, clanking dishes, and silverware.

When it was late and Dad hadn't come home, I'd find her standing by the back door, her head resting on the glass in the top half. She'd puff on her cigarette. Then she'd pick the skin off her lower lip with her fingernails. And stare out the door window. I never knew what she was seeing, or if she saw anything.

I'd stand for a while, watching her. I'd wait for it. It always came. The sigh. First her chest would rise higher and then her back seemed to stretch out and then I heard the rush of air, saw her breath fogging the glass. Her sigh seemed like steam puffing out of a pressure canner. My grandmother once told me that a pressure canner builds up steam and you have to let it off eventually, or it will explode.

When I was too hungry to wait any longer, I'd say, "Mommy?" No answer. "Mommy, I'm hungry." And then she'd turn and look down at me and she'd say, "Sit down." I'd sit down in my usual chair, and she spooned food on my plate. She wouldn't eat with me. She'd say, "I'll wait till your daddy gets in." I knew it might be a long time before she ate. She'd return to the door, more deep inhales, slow exhales, but it seemed to me no pressure was released. Was it amour? No, it didn't seem so.

The pattern of waiting, watching, sighing, repeated through my childhood, my teens. Even after I left home at 19. My mom, sighing her way through life, waiting on my dad to change his stripes, to come home sober. The day she stopped sighing was the day the pressure became too great. The waiting, all sad-eyed, staring out the window became crying in a hospital ward bed, where they worked to get my mother to remember to breathe.

Patricia Thrushart

Wise Admonishments

I never wanted to grow dahlias.
All that effort—digging them up
before hard frost,
letting the clinging dirt dry,
painting nicks with sulphur,
packing tubers in cushioning moss.

Too fussy for this avant-garde gardener!
Shouldn't plants scrape by if put
in a decent enough place?
But a friend gave me dahlias and
a wise admonishment: be ruthless.

This is the real hardship of dahlias:
cutting them down
at their most voluptuous.

Shei Sanchez

Sunday afternoon sitting by the Hocking

this family of mine lies cradled by sun and shadow,
by crisp leaves above cool earth. Their mouths

moving masticated forbs and grasses
in four-four time. Sometimes, in accidental unison.

Others times, like this moment, when I pretend
my goats are maestros in canon. Young phenoms

chanting Row, Row, Row Your Boat,
delighting their mum with the newest discovery

of being children. The parent buried in me
grips her heart, swallows back memory's cry.

A vision of motherhood was swallowed long ago.
Down that went into the whirlpool

of expectations, illness, time. A decade
of penitent rain and tender skies made up for them.

These past two years, I have time-traveled
with my kids to the tale-ridden places

of our home. Castles in the shape
of sandstone boulders. Bottomless hollows

that carve ditties to dancing trees.
Streams and creeks that baptize valleys

with new names. At each page, we stop
and wait for the lessons.

With every strike of the clock,
I hear the river's refrain.

There is no turning back.

Shei Sanchez

A Made Thing

Waist-deep, we were,
   in fescue and foxtail,
in that fresh falling
   into something

close enough
   to a made thing
called fire.
   That soft kindling

stars are made of—
   a wild light
aflame
   in everything

we touched.
   White and burr oaks
swooned.
   American columbo
blossomed.

The lone cedar
   and wood thrush
in the hollow
   did not feel such

solitude anymore.
   The forest deepened
her green for us
   that day, as if

she knew how
   to fill a cup
that burns
   for brightness.

Helga Kidder

Dragonfly

Swimming in late afternoon,
I watch the devil's darning needle
hover like a helicopter
over the pool. His wings beat
so slowly, I hear the sizzle
of his weightless ballet
before he skims the salty blue
like a kamikaze fighter.

He could be an alien
visiting earth with his stained-glass
body and see-through wings
as he continues to sample
the garden's smorgasbord
of flies, wasps, moths.
His chain of ancestry
longer than the dinosaur's
in the warming of the world.

As I part the velvety water
tinged with light,
not a stone is unturned
in the grace of creation.
While he sews odd pieces of air
into the day's quilt,
he drains surplus of whatever
he carries on his shoulders,
as we do when watching nature.
But sometimes, as if blind-folded,
we don't see the miracles
unfolding in front of our eyes.

Sue Weaver Dunlap

Pondering Passion

Love moves gentle across rain-wet clothes. Drops gather speed,
two bodies reach, faces skyward, rivers pooling over love. Front
yard green twined tight our nakedness below mountain's fullest clouds.

Snow settles deep. Afternoon holler walk brings us to pine thickets
burdened with snow. Quiet glazes our center, a season for love. Glass
crystals dot our hair. Pressed close, our skin buries us, our breaths warmed.

Hay bales stacked high early June. One hundred reunions of sweat
and arms hoisting fodder for winter. Storms rise fast, our shelter sweet
warm hay. Thunder rolls high up. Our spines dissolve. Dust pelts our sighs.

Crinkled skin wakes our love communion, now when dusty rose
petals fall away like the years we inscribed our fervor, love patterns
in morning porch sitting, days shorter, breathing memories of young love.

Sue Weaver Dunlap

Bathed in Dew

My face spoke to morning sun's fullness
our waking minute aligned. We crawled
from slumber, yawned into day's chores
no early morning chatter, no earth noise
until first light touched our garden patch.
I floated barefoot deep in grass dew

heavy under touch. I hand cupped dew
to wash away lingering night, felt fullness
of the day, thought to weed the corn patch
before summer heat cracked. Hope crawled
deep. My heart calloused against noise
in a shotgun house, hunger and chores

to feed when copper-laced ground chores
burdened on us all, and I wished the dew
was heavy enough to wash away the noise
of hunger, Mommy's breasts dead, fullness
gone like the day James Marion crawled
against her and died, buried in a patch

behind the house, him wrapped in a patch
quilt large enough to hold two, a chore
for Mommy to tend to others, she crawled
inside her grief and cried tears thick as dew
I ran my hands through, its sweet fullness
feeding me enough to block the noise

of young desire. Death rattles cold noise
in my own quilt of shame, a baby to patch
quiet loss while I grieve his soft fullness
along my face of tears. Morning chores
hold our baby close asleep, cold lover, dew
across his red clay blanket where I crawled

this late July day, time tripped and crawled
closer to quiet me. I turned against noise,
left love behind on far mountain. Dew
cries for me now, my own tears a patch

of earth at the back of Zion Hill. Chores
follow me. Hope fell away, its fullness
trapped in dew. Love closed. I crawled,
wept his fullness, his scent of faint noise,
a patch of him growing, burdened chores.

Lynette Ford

Lost Treasure

She speaks with her eyes.
Her word is fear.
I respond with a polished lie:
This will be okay.
Then I offer her the only truth I can:
I love you.
A tear escapes, sparkles, a diamond
clutched at the corner of her perception,
the facets of her world cut smaller
as she loses the treasure of herself.

Lynette Ford

Because They're Wild

I let weeds grow because they're wild.

They make no apology, offer no explanations.
They are beauty with no expectation
except to freely live
unframed for the beholder's eye.

I thank the hills for such gifts,
for wise ways, medicines and mysteries.
I'm sorry that I, living here, impose upon their lives.
Untouched, what magic might such flowers become?

Some people curate a sense of beauty
from a single tea rose point of view,
then find little comfort in the concrete canyons
and false mountains they call home.

Meanwhile,
wildflowers bloom.
Leaf beetles and bees find fortune's treasure
in a growth of sweet Joe-Pye.

Hummingbirds shudder over columbines.
Butterflies drift on lavender winds,
nurtured by what was beautiful long before
the judgment of seeded lawn and garden style.

Connie Jordan Green

Hawk

—after Deborah Warren

Air is his occupation, and the hawk
rides thermals like a trapeze artist

swinging from handhold to handhold,
the sun his only companion—the sun

and an occasional crow tormenting
him away from a nest of hatchlings.

I've watched the hawk on a summer
afternoon, flash of red beneath his tail

as he banks, his flight pure joy, making
of the day what can be made of light

and buoyancy. As for me, my habitat
is earth, feet firmly planted, gravity

my rule—but the imagination, where
we all live, learns its own aerobatics,

knows flight, the joy of hawk and
of crow, how all can soar and yet find

a place on a sheet of paper, a home
in a poem taking flight across the page.

Connie Jordan Green

Morning Song

I will rise as the eastern sky shows day's
first pink stain, and I will step outdoors
and be glad for another day on this tiny
planet hurtling through space, and I will try
to remember how luck has brought me here,

from the billions of unborn souls—
innumerable sperm and egg unjoined—
the unimaginable odds that created
you and me, how the void we move toward
day after day, is no worse than the void

we once inhabited, and I will note the trees
filled with green leaves or a patchwork
in fall or winter's forsaken bare limbs reaching
for the sky, and I will go about my life of chore
and rest, of sorrow and of praise, and I will be glad.

Connie Jordan Green

Moving to the Country

It was our first winter on the farm,
twenty-five-year-olds with a one-year
old, another on the way. The farmhouse
was small, uninsulated, a cold water
spigot in the kitchen, light bulb dangling
from the ceiling in each of the four rooms,
no heating system. We added a bath
in the corner of the kitchen, wrapped

the windows and back porch in plastic,
piled firewood on the front porch,
and hunkered down. Mid-October,
cold set in, temperatures started
a slow slide that would last into
late March. In early December, water
froze in the toilet bowl, snow swirled
around the house. All winter wind

moaned in the chimney, bent the cedars
like hapless wanderers bowing
in supplication before a god that paid
no mind to anyone's troubles. When
the first daffodil popped through spring's
thawing soil, we emerged into a world
we had forgotten existed—warm sun
on our faces like the kiss of a long-lost lover.

Jessica Manack

Archaeology

We may as well have been Columbus, da Gama,
my brother and I, born into a world they called New:
pastless, plastic, no photos on the walls, only
tchotchkes on the mantels, only our fairy tales.
We lived in a suburb sprung up around the airport,
history-free, formerly farms.

We played outside in those days, banished
to the kids' kingdom, so Mom could have her Stories,
Days, One Life to Live, sharing a play-by-play
with her sister over the phone. Other peoples' stories.
Our shadowy corners were something to
peroxide, to hide, create antidotes against.

We made potions, mixed berries and petals.
The hydrangeas bloomed their aluminum blue.
We dug in the dirt in our yard, one day
unearthing trash 1940s fires had failed to burn,
small glass vials, metal toothpaste tubes.
We learned that people here had been wilder,

only recently imposing the suburban order.
In metal barrels the trash burned out back,
secrets vanishing quicker than S'mores.
We spread out our evidence, asking questions.
Who had been here before? Why had they left?
What brought us here? What kept us here?

We didn't know our mother didn't even know
her grandmother was alive, confined to an asylum.
We didn't know our grandmother's teenage
pregnancy was the reason her family moved
three states away one summer, sudden East-coasters.
We only knew stories burbled under the surface,

noses poking up through the seafoam.
Baby detectives, we were unquenchable,
skeptical, magnifying-glassed, leaving no junk
drawer unemptied, finding what there was to find.
We scratched and scrabbled and scoured,
asking only, if we hadn't been meant to know,
would we have been fitted with these little claws?

Karen Salyer McElmurray

Spirit House

1. River

I once saw a spirit house as I rode a tour boat along the Chao Phraya River in Bangkok. A shikara took us past temples and markets, past high-rise malls and the high, nasal notes of Thai pop music, past docks and hawker's stalls, past a clamor of people, people. We slowed as we came to tall iron gates surrounding a terraced garden. Inside was a huge dwelling and beside it, atop tall columns, were two much smaller houses. *Guardians of the spirit,* our guide said. *Blessed by holy men.* One spirit house guarded wealth and the other the ancestors. Inset with red, blue, yellow, and silver glass, the houses sparkled in the morning sunlight pushing its way through the smog-filled air of Bangkok.

2. Get Them Here

Over the years, I have seen spirit houses for sale for anywhere from fifty bucks to five hundred. *Get your best deals on spirit houses and shop the largest selections,* Ebay says. Some of these spirit houses have would-be spires and simulated stained glass windows. They are table size. Palm size. Made of teak, gold glass, balsam and painted mirrors.

The spirit house I used to have is small—a blue-painted one that I bought at a road-side sale in Eastern Kentucky. The table I stopped at was laden with the houses—bright colors, some covered in moons and stars. At first as I walked the length of the table I thought they were bird houses. A man selling them had one eye and a voice that held a laugh as he picked up a red and yellow house and held it out to me. *You can hold them houses up to the wind and about hear your people pray*, the man said.

3. Spirit Inside

After my friend Linda died in the early months of the pandemic, I helped with clearing out her room. I had met Linda a couple of years back while walking my dog, and we developed a friendship over coffee and conversations about Mark, her boyfriend of some twenty years. Mark didn't care that Linda had no resources of her own. He didn't care that Linda couldn't work, and he failed to grasp what a stroke meant. Partial paralysis on her left side. Fear of being alone in the dark. The room Linda rented after Mark kicked her out when he met someone? Ten by nine, with just a bed. On the free space of floor, there were plates with half-eaten sandwiches, unopened Hostess pies. A closet was jam-packed with everything, including a spirit house. It was sculpture made of barn wood I remembered seeing in Linda's former flower garden, and I took it home with me. I think about how it captured her spirit those pandemic days. Her, huddled up in the bed with her laptop, streaming her soaps, the story after story where everything works out in the end.

4. Phuket

By the time we reached southern Thailand, we'd been traveling for almost a year—France, Greece, Australia, India—travels with no more purpose than the next town, the next country. We'd walked the humid districts of Bangkok, bought discount CD players and headphones to resell when we reached India. We'd quarreled about the best money changing rate as we slept in cheap and good guest houses. We finally took a bus north to Chang Mai, in a hostel that looked across the river to Burma. There, we ate blood-streaked eggs from the mangy hens that ran past the hostel. We lay beneath the mosquito netting over our separate beds as our quarrels grew and grew, alongside our plans to head to the sea to lick our wounds.

In southern Thailand, in Phuket, I tried being alone on for size. I walked miles each day. I swam out to the tall rock formations rising from the ocean, my fingers lingering on sea algae and the small mouths of anemone. I hiked deep into the rainforest, past a tree house where a monk had left his orange robe. Found a Buddhist temple where I prayed to no one particular god. I knelt before burning incense and photographs of surgeries—bodies cut open at chest or abdomen, missing eyes or limbs. Beside me, nuns knelt in prayer as if the photographs were offerings to the divine. By dusk, I was back with you and we ate bowls of salty dumplings. At night, in a grass hut beside the sea, its windows propped open in the stifling air, we touched as little as possible.

Sleeping, I breathed into the total darkness of a Phuket night. Breathing, I slept and I traveled. Traveled along a path near the sea, next to smooth boulders and whorl-leaved she-oaks. My breath traveled until it reached a garden fragrant with jasmine, traveled until it stopped beside a house no bigger than a spread wide palm. Breath entered the windows of that small spirit house. Breath swept the tiny floors clean, laid breath-hands against the small bare walls. Breath rested until I was rested and like that, I traveled west. I crossed continents and oceans. My breath was not as afraid as I myself was of finding a place called home.

5. Names of Spirit Houses

Smoke house. Canning house. Chicken coop. Warm house. Long house. Hog pen. Coal shed. House at Lynch. House at Lancer. House in Allen. House in Dwale. House in Hagerhill. House in Mining Hollow. House in Prestonsburg. House in Paintsville. Brown house. White house. Green and white trailer house. House with a fireplace where the coal ghosts travel up in smoke. House with a trunk found behind a wall. House with glass-eyed dolls. House with quilts. House of the Holy Spirit. House of the Resurrection. House of voices raised in praise. House after the flood. House of bones. House forgotten. House remembered. House-that-travels-through-time. Goodbye house. House of my heart. House now that can never be house then.

6. Abandoned House

On the road to Assateague National Park, there's a field where I once photographed an abandoned house. Two-storied, used-to-be white, broken windows and a door off its hinges, a roof sliding off into the grass. I circled this house, prodding with my toe at tin cans and a rusted barrel full of trash and an old blue iodine bottle I put in my pack.

Inside the place smelled like age-old dust and my phone lit up the walls, glowing with red and black and yellow shapes. UFO's and aliens and devils. Power fists and words. *Art makes right. Deconstruct this.* The house had been visited by William Blake. Skinny red angels floated, their palms open, their faces with distorted mouths. Down a long hall was a broken window and through it came the sound of meadow, bees and the call of ocean birds. In a bedroom, a rusted bed frame was like one at a grandmother's house when I was little. I remembered jumping, the give and creak of springs, and some voice telling me to quit that now. I closed my eyes and waited to see if they were in this place, the spirits of these ancestors.

7. Hunger

Ghosts residing in Thai spirit houses are hungry, and they are left offerings as appeasement. Coconuts. Bananas. Sticky rice and custard. Once, at the end of a trash-strewn alley in the center of Bangkok, I saw a simple spirit house made of woven straw and tin scraps, a piece of plywood as its platform. Someone had left brown eggs and mango slices gone to an orangey syrup atop rice cakes. Traffic and a tangle of street voices in the distance, I knelt. In the midst of the offerings was a burner, an unlit stick of incense and a small photograph. A girl-child in the arms of a woman with haunted eyes. At the foot of the photo was an opened can of red Fanta soda. Later, I read that red soda is the equivalent of a blood offering.

8. Where Spirits Reside

On the top of the shelf is an altar. Objects I love. A piece of jade. Shells from Assateague. Tiny clay cups and bowl filled with pebbles from Alaska. There are representations of the Holy Mother. A Black Madonna from Spain. A hand carved Mary from Turkey. A small icon of Mary and her son, from Russia. The truly religious parts of the altar are photographs. There's my great-grandmother, Beck, sitting in a booth at The Black Cat diner, smoking her pipe. There's my father, his arm draped across my shoulders, that time I did my first public reading from a memoir. There's his mother, my mother, her mother, her mother before her.

Below the altar, shelves are crammed with books. Poetry. Volumes on magic and the occult. Meditations. Thomas Merton's *Seven Story Mountain* is there, as is Rilke's *Book of Hours*. There's *Women of the Golden Dawn*. *The Tibetan Book of the Dead.* A King James Bible from my childhood. When I was a child, I wrote names of those born and those who'd passed in that King James Bible. As I grow older these days, I am less sure about what truths I can write down, which truths it's possible to hold onto as years turn into decades. Mothers and grandmothers, fathers and daughters. And all these things shall pass away. A spirit house.

9. Things Spirits Have Blessed

Magnifying glass. Kerosene lamp. 78 rpm records. Crochet hooks. Lace doilies. Milking stool. Trip around the World Quilt. Lead crystal perfume bottle. Cast iron kettle. Iodine bottle. Carved wooden salt shakers. Hagerhill Community Cookbook. Garnet wedding ring, band worn thin with wear. Log Cabin Quilt. Straight razor with ivory handle. Band saw. Deed to forty acres. Candlewick saucers. Small knife, blade thin as paper. Wedding Ring Quilt. Rusty steel cheese grater. Green glass lemon juicer. Embroidered pillow cases. Wooden handled hammer. Needle, thread, scissors, cloth. A windup mantel clock that no longer works.

10. Soup Bowl

I came back to the United States with my backpack stuffed full. Folded inside my tee shirts were stones and bones and feathers from France and Greece and India. From India itself there were two papier-mache boxes from Kashmir, sandstones from Agra, a pair of pointy slippers from Rajasthan. From Thailand there was one gift only—a beautiful blue and white lidded soup tureen.

When I now visit my stepmother, who lives alone since my father died, we watch movies with happy endings. When she goes in to take her evening bath, I look at her curio cabinet, full of her sacred objects. Photos of her grandfather. Stuffed animals. A brush for lathering a face. At the bottom of the curio cabinet is that china soup tureen from Thailand, and I take it out, hold it like a talisman.

I bought it in a high-rise super mall in Bangkok, on a table laden with silk scarves, animal carvings, and miniature paintings of Phuket and Chang Mai. Now I take its gold-edged lid off and peer down into the tureen, thinking about how it's never been used, never held spicy broths and shrimp, glassy noodles and garlic and vegetables. It's a keepsake.

I reach inside, feel the cool china sides. The bottom of the tureen seems endless. I reach and reach, and my hand disappears, then my arm, and I close my eyes, letting all of me follow. I am a spirit now, following a china path back and back. A spirit self, I step into air, into sky, into space and times before. I am standing in my spirit self at the steps leading up into a temple with a golden Buddha. I am holding my lover's hand and it feels dry and rough, though he, too, is nothing but spirit now, after all these years. Spirits, we stand listening to the chants of the monks, the singing bowls that invite us to make ourselves comfortable.

11. Graves

In Prestonsburg, on the way toward Lancer, is a community cemetery. There are gravestones for Leroy and Pearlie Baisden. For Ruby Lafferty. Up Mining Hollow, at a smaller family cemetery, there's Ruth, Dave and Greg Campbell. Off 23, toward Paintsville, there's another cemetery where Pearlie Lee Baisden lies. Outside Paintsville, another family cemetery. In the proliferation of wild roses and ivy lie Fanny and Clarence Salyer. Ida Mae and John Salyer. Up the holler outside East Point, there are graves I don't even know. Great-grandfather. Great-grandmother. And in the waters of Dewey Lake, at Jenny Wiley, the ashes of Clarence Edsel Salyer have fed the fish. When I stand outside at night at the edge of the lake and watch moonrise, I make myself listen, listen. The barking of dogs. An owl. A whippoorwill. Spirits, glad to be spirits. How the wind sings down the mountains.

12. The body

In the hall, I stand in front of the mirror, studying my naked body. Behind me the photos of my ancestors whisper and laugh. They point it out to me, how my body is changing year by year. Breasts descending, stomach a soft pouch, hips rounder. My hands show the years of jobs that meant shovel and rake, and I see Willy May, my great-grandfather, in those hands. My face, wrinkles on the forehead, shadows beneath the eyes, is my mother's. Ghost of her smile in my smile, her laughter rising from my throat. Look at yourself, the spirits say. I fear this aging body, but I look.

Mine is a body gone from the land of its ancestors more years than it can count. A forty years journey away from home. Daughter of Pearlie Lee Baisden, from Dwale, and Clarence Edsel Salyer, from Allen, this body wanted more. Wanted distant countries, towns, cities. Wanted highways and interstates that led away and away. Where the body came from became a dim light on some front porch. Became the memory of a voice in the dark calling me home. This body forgotten the substance of kith and kin, and the open arms to welcome this stranger home have become fewer and fewer. You are becoming, the spirits say, a vessel for what is missing.

Cool air from a vent blows down on my skin. I want to believe air is palpable, a thing I can catch and release. I want to believe spirits are not things, but sign of the lives before us, the lives we have lived, and will live, forever and forever, amen. My hands catch the air, bring the sweet taste to my mouth. The air is full of spirits, so many I have known and loved, so many I have loved without that knowing. Mother, father, uncles, aunts. I take them inside me, one by one by one. I give them the only house I have for now.

Ellis Elliott

Appalachian Triolet

(Granny Grills)

Continents yawned and spilled oceans
once, ancient shoreline, my backyard
of silver scales, salt for potions.
Continents yawned and spilled oceans,
offerings of bones, rare tokens
for conjuring, lifting life's scars.
Continents yawned and spilled oceans
once, ancient shoreline, my backyard.

Ellis Elliott

Peculiar

(Granny Grills)

Daniel says I come from peculiar, an ancient breed
makers of tinctures and tins of odorous salves in myriad hues.
I say I come from torn sky on pitch mountain nights

when the veil of stars lifts like valley fog and I can see
beyond this weighted world, where his rooted boots stay.
Daniel, I say I am right peculiar, from an ancient breed

they call a Granny Woman. I'm a healer and leaf reader,
receiver of gifts from the Divine, practical tools
I say comes from torn sky on pitch mountain nights,

when the messages taste like chimney smoke, and remedies
sing from the leaves of sumac and sweetfern.
Daniel says I'm from peculiar ancient breeds

of grandmothers, his ancestors anchored in Cherokee
and Celt customs spoken and bequeathed. Daniel,
I say come in from your torn sky on pitch mountain nights

to rest by the hearth and heal, feed in the flickering light
of fire and moon, and the amber of hot turtlehead tea.
Daniel says I come from peculiar, an ancient breed
from torn sky on mountain nights. Come in I say.

Ellis Elliott

Scrawl

(Granny Grills)

Sometimes I can't find God in the scrawl
of blue mountains around me, try as I might to pull
a bucket of sense from the well of the earth
to pour floods on the fires of war

in the blue mountains around me, I might pull
bulbs to brew, chant verses, conjure storms
that pour, then flood. The fires of war
roll from the hills into homes, women holler

for my bulbs to brew, chant verses, conjure storms
as balm for raw palms, light to drink the darkness
rolling from hills into homes, women holler
over sickbeds, small coffins, mothers

are balm for raw palms, light that drinks darkness,
buckets of sense from the well of the earth.
Mothers holler over sickbeds, small coffins,
and sometimes I can't find God in the scrawl.

Leatha Kendrick

Dear Solitude,

dear house of only me, dear
branches leafing through a windowed sky
and no thought of meals to cook
or money in the bank,
                   dear morning
waking alone and delicious, dear freedom
from fear of what I might say, might
have already said to indict myself,
                       dear
time without everyone I love, dear what I am
afraid to want so much for fear
I'll get it, dear children I miss who don't
need me around, dear thoughts
slower to come,
              dear muted flesh,
dear black pit, dear refusal,
dear how-did-I-end-up-here? and dear
confusion uncertain whether
what it wants is worth
getting up for,
                  dear husband bringing me
a second cup of coffee, dear hushed inner self,
dear singing, please come back, show me again
how to make a place for you,
                dear room,
let me claim more than four walls, let mornings
come, let the tree across the street

teach me again how slow
leafing and unleafing are, let stillness

claim the hours, let them be filled
again with nothing

but words that rise
into silence.

Leatha Kendrick

Mangle

Even at 8 I knew that meant
arm in the corn picker,
somebody's body rent,
blood and bone, by moving metal.

But this mangle, docile, dozed
next to her kitchen table, swallowed
sheets and pillowcases fed into its rollers.

It ticked and waited. Curved back
stolid as a cow. Sometimes it hissed
and spit—like a train or angry cat.
Her fingers flashed at its maw

each wash day, regular as seams,
as rows of beans. Calm as lake water,
she worked its jaws with a lever, with her knees.

She was lithe then, in her 50's, her energy
still strong. She taught us how
to iron and make a bed. She showed
us how to sew on buttons, hem and mend.

She made sure we learned needlework. She gave
us art and read to us, and then she taught us
to play cards—canasta, pinochle.

She ran a tight ship, starched her husband's
heavy khaki pants and his work shirts. She ran
the iron's hot point around the patch on the chest—
Otto H. Romann, Case Farm Equipment Dealership.

Tucked in the kitchen's corner, her Maytag
sloshed and mumbled to itself.
Her dryer whirred, whirled.

She had her own machines. She
kept everything oiled.

Leatha Kendrick

A brown bird

dips and flits in a brown
recess among the dying
boughs of cryptomeria. Sparrow,

but what kind, I have not yet pinned down.
Today it is her brown that sets
the yard to rights. A not-dying,

a motion like breath, like guests
perched for a while on the patio's
uncomfortable teak chairs,

knees bent, arms folded in
to lift a glass of wine, to stay
awhile and fill us up with talk.

Gone now, the ones who sat,
but the sparrow's come
and I'm content. The rusty
spikes of evergreen die off,
the tree lives around the opened
        spaces.

Jayne Moore Waldrop

Deliverance

Five hours south by southeast
a break from the world awaits,
a gift of time and space to write
read hike listen think in a studio
of my own, a place surrounded
by woods and flowers
at the end of a gravel road,
a cabin with a skylight
and clerestory for letting in
daylight and views of swaying
treetops, or a full moon beaming
like a searchlight around
unadorned white walls,
and on clear, quiet nights a star
that twinkles right above the bed.

Before my arrival some kind soul
had placed two stems of iris
in a plain glass vase on the desk—
one tall bearded pale yellow,
the other Siberian deep purple.
All week the array evolves
as one bloom shines then
begins to fade, takes its bow,
closes into a tight little knot
and is soon replaced by fresh
beauty up or down the fleshy,
green stalk. An emerging blossom
takes centerstage, vibrant, alive,
like its predecessor once looked—
was that just yesterday?

One by one the buds work
to unfurl, to become what they
were meant to be, and then fade,
taking turns from yellow to purple,
all yellow, one exquisite purple,
sometimes a solo performance,
maybe two or three at once

bursting into a chorus of color,
sometimes nothing, the stem
standing bare naked until the next
bloom is ready to deliver, in rhythm
with the others that came before,
like a metronome keeping time
for my words until the last flower
drops and I leave for home.

Rita Sims Quillen

A Sort of Autobiography

I am not easy in any way,
    never smooth or quietly efficient.
I am not neat or orderly—my life
    is a spilled salad scooped back in the bowl.
I have never been popular or admired,
    only pitied like a roadside kitten.

I do not want jewelry or plastic surgery,
    as my daily faces of contentment and peace
    are quite enough falseness.
I do not know where to stand at parties
    or how to hide a runaway pulse.
I have no concept of finesse,
    no ability to navigate swift shallows.
I cannot cross a log-breached creek
    or make delicate pie crusts
    or say the right thing to the grieving.

I don't speak frankly ever
    only slantwise truths with downcast eyes
    off balance down to sinew and vein.
The world soaks up my words like a bandage
    invisible blood staining the day.

Rita Sims Quillen

What Bees Say

When I visit the park, my babies ghost it.
Little people entertaining each other
blind to the world, so noisy nothing breaks their din.
All grown up, far and far away from me now
they no longer breach the silence.
It's such a deep quiet
I not only hear but feel
the heavy bee swarm to my right,
a white-hot energy humming on a low branch.
Their loud pulse is a fugue of worry,
collective frantic panic:
Will we still be us tomorrow?

When there's no way back to where we were,
we must swarm out on meadows' breath.
Bees form their tightest knot
when silent air signals the world is broken.
They smother each other with hope
once the center is gone.

Nature knows well how to rewind
but wastes no energy there,
knows all about recriminations, regrets
the replays and reprises but holds
those echoes from evening's soft call.
No shadows or ghosts in bee tree or fox den.
Stop looking back, tempting a salty fate,
the hum says.
You were never meant to be a pillar.

Rita Sims Quillen

Three Times I Addressed the Moon as Jesus

—Denial: "Thy sun shall no more go down; neither shall thy moon withdraw itself: for the Lord shall be thine everlasting light, and the days of thy mourning shall be ended." (Isaiah 60:20)

Three times I addressed the moon
after they said brother was on the ventilator,
stepped out into the night
so I could cry and beg in peace,
shocked to see the framed centered painting
of her ancient face
bright as the searchlight
of heaven's night watchman on cold shoreline
out my front door.

—Anger: "For the stars of heaven and the constellations thereof shall not give their light: the sun shall be darkened in his going forth, and the moon shall not cause her light to shine." (Isaiah 13-10)

I raged and seethed
demanding this cup to pass,
for another Lazarus moment yet again
after several already granted.
Surely the game would not end this way,
like Jesus ran a blackjack table
and could palm us some cards.

—Bargaining: "He appointed the moon for seasons: the sun knoweth his going down." (Psalm 104:19)

Addressing her a second night,
I apologized for yelling,
for banging my cup on the bars,
for demanding someone endure torment
so as not to upset my world,
like life was some roadside vegetable stand
and I could expect God
to put his thumb on the scale
adding to the final tally in my purse.

—*Depression: "Tomorrow is the new moon, and thou shalt be missed, because thy seat will be empty." (1 Samuel 20:18)*

The third visit was silent,
edge beginning to blacken on the face—
but what remained shone clearer.
Tears were not torrents this time.
her beam softer in the summer haze
but black night and white face
sign and portent
not to be missed,
stark relief of the eternal
beaming out to me
from ages past
for just this moment.

—*Acceptance: "There is one glory of the sun and another glory of the moon, and another glory of the stars: for one star differeth from another star in glory." (1 Corinthians 15-41)*

Since I know his spirit watches over me
I stand mute now before the solitary,
silent because I am alone
no longer singing at the sky like a warrior
heading into battle.
Warriors sang themselves unto death
answering siren song from the other side,
from the white noise of the face
out my front door.
Tonight, I am dry as bone
moon face hidden behind the curtain
of stars and dark energy,
that blank slate
now carried inside
heavy as stone.

Erin Miller Reid

The Ways They Go

Martha would never forget the Sunday morning she told Sandra P.J. had died. She'd never forget the way Sandra crumpled to the floor, never forget the animal moan that surged from her daughter's throat, never forget how Saturday night's leftover mascara blackened Sandra's cheeks.

Martha and Miriam had raised Sandra and P.J. together, more like cousins than just friends, carting them to Sunday school and tee-ball games, spending whole summer afternoons stirring pitchers of grape Kool-Aid and watching the two of them splash in a plastic baby pool in the backyard.

Martha was with Miriam the morning the deputy dropped off a black Hefty sack of P.J.'s belongings. Miriam uncinched the bag's plastic tie, and she and Martha peeked inside. The metallic odor of iron and the musk of a teenage boy hit them immediately. Miriam had staggered backwards and caught herself on the stair banister. Martha knotted the bag and set it on the back porch. "You can decide later what you want to do with it," she told her friend. Martha wondered how a mother could make that decision—throw away your boy's things like they were garbage or scrub them out and watch rust-tinged suds from your dead son's bloodied clothing wash down the drain.

When Martha thought about the details, she wanted to vomit into the nearest commode. The loss of anyone, especially a young person, was devastating, but she couldn't abide the loss of P.J. The thing about that boy was that he was going to make something of himself. P.J. Sutton was one of the few kids who would've actually left Wickers Bend. Smart, athletic, got along with just about everyone, had a full college scholarship, and, unlike most of the other kids in the county, his parents made sure he knew more than how to dress a deer, strip tobacco, and quote Proverbs. The Sutton house brimmed with books—on shelves, on the coffee table, under end tables. Martha borrowed books from Miriam instead of checking them out from the library since the Suttons didn't charge late fees. The family visited art museums where they'd seen actual van Goghs, Monets, and even the painting of the farmer with a pitchfork standing next to his wife. They bought tickets to the orchestra in Lexington and Knoxville.

Heeding the Sutton family's example, Martha had once taken Sandra to see *Cats*. She'd worn her nicest Sunday dress and made Sandra do the same. In downtown Knoxville, Martha cussed the drivers that honked their horns at her as she attempted to navigate the one-way streets. She and Sandra had to walk eight blocks in pumps from the only parking space she found that didn't cost two hours of Raymond's wages. By the time they got to the theater, Martha's armpits were ringed in sweat and her bangs were plastered to her forehead. "Puttin' petals on an onion, don't make it a rose," her mama would've chided. Martha had loved every minute of that performance though—the gilded, corniced balconies of the theater, the actors' elaborate face paint, the disco lights, the way, at the very end, Grizabella rose to the sky on a spaceship hubcap in swirls of smoke. Sandra left the theater with stars in her eyes, vowing she'd move to New York so she could see Broadway shows every weekend. The declaration triggered a twinge in the center of Martha's chest.

Art and concerts. Books and church. A mother that cooked square meals and a father who taught him to how to pound a nail and save money. P.J. would have made it out of Wickers Bend and made something of himself.

Martha had almost made it out of Wickers Bend herself once. The Class of 1964 voted her *Most Likely to Succeed*. When she told her parents, her mama said, "Don't get no big notions, missy." Her daddy had only chuckled, amused, as if she were still a little girl trying to walk in his clunky work boots.

Martha applied to college in Louisville the spring of her senior year. She wrote the entrance essay and even arranged boarding. When she received the acceptance letter, her daddy wouldn't speak to her and her mama cried for days, shuffling around the house with a tissue in the pocket of her housecoat, sniffling whenever she looked at Martha. "Wickers Bend needs its young people. The church needs you. Your family needs you." Raymond penned a letter pledging his love. He wrote that he'd already picked out land for them just two hills over from her parents if she'd stay and marry him.

Martha hitched a ride to the bus stop in town anyway, a baloney sandwich and Raymond's letter in her pocketbook. As she waited, she swore she could feel the ink of Raymond's words burning through the leather of her purse, singeing the skin of her thigh. She swore she could smell the love of her disappointed mother seeping from between the two slices of the baloney sandwich. The fumes of an idling Greyhound choked her as she tried to resist the magnetic draw of the payphone. She felt like a failure when she broke down and called her daddy for a ride home. Teary-eyed, she picked at the pilled threads of her skirt the whole silent drive back to Wickers Bend. She married Raymond the next summer.

Martha might not have made it out, and poor P.J. hadn't, but Martha was determined that Sandra would leave Wickers Bend. The college semester started in two weeks, and Martha had spent June and July making sure her daughter was ready to leave home. She took Sandra to town to open a bank account and taught her to balance a checkbook. She carted her to the Laundromat twelve miles down 25W to make sure she knew how to manage those coin-fed machines. While waiting for a dryer, she showed Sandra how to fold a fitted sheet.

"Mom, you worry about everything," Sandra had said.

"Because anything can happen, and you need to be ready for it." For the past two months, Martha had cycled through every *what if* she could conjure, from strange roommates and failed tests to bad boyfriends and keg parties.

This afternoon she'd teach Sandra to change the tire of a car. Sandra waited for her in the driver's seat with the windows rolled down, listening to the radio.

"Sis, you're gonna kill the battery doing that," Martha opened the driver's door for her daughter to get out, wondering how Sandra still lacked so much common sense. Martha fished the spare tire, the jack, and the lug wrench from the trunk, and then knelt next to the tan Ford Taurus that Raymond had bought for their daughter at the used car lot. She cranked the jack to raise the car's frame.

Sandra stood behind Martha, tracing a line in the dirt with the wooden toe of her sandal. "Use this lug wrench to unscrew the tire." Martha muscled the metal rod back and forth to loosen the screws, then plinked them into the bowl of the upturned cap. "Now, just slide it off, and then put on the spare."

"Yes, Mama." Sandra shifted side to side, only her denim cut-offs and tanned legs visible from Martha's kneeling position on the ground. Some of that tan was from Sandra's job bringing in tobacco, but the girl had also spent too many idle afternoons slathered in baby oil and iodine sweltering under the sun on an old quilt in the backyard.

"Always make sure you've got a spare tire," Martha thumped the tire with her fist, "And remember, you can't drive too far or too fast on it."

A car barreled up the drive, honking and stirring up a cloud of dust. Nirvana blared from the rolled down windows. Martha rose to her feet, palm flat across her brow to shield the sun.

"It's Gina," Sandra waved at her friend. A teenage blonde with oversized sunglasses poked her head from the gravel-dusted Camaro. "Wanna go to the spillway, Sandra?" Sandra cocked her head towards Martha, eyes pleading.

Martha sighed. "Go ahead." Both girls whooped as Sandra grabbed her two-piece and a towel from the clothesline.

Martha wiped the grease and sweat from her hands onto the hips of her denim Bermuda shorts. "You girls be careful," she hollered well after the car was out of earshot. After this summer, after losing P.J., Martha's admonition to be careful carried more heft, more consequence.

Martha thought back to when the kids were little. Raymond and Dr. Sutton had bush-hogged a path through the tall field of grass a half-mile between their properties. They mowed the path weekly so that Sandra and P.J. had easy access to each other's houses without having to take the road. Martha would stand on the back porch and watch Sandra until her head disappeared over the edge of the hill swallowed by the wispy ends of foxtail grass. Martha longed for those days when all she had to do was to cut a path from point A to point B to keep Sandra safe, when P.J. was still alive at the other end of that path. Martha gazed down the hill toward the Sutton house. It looked lifeless. Before, Miriam had always left the front door open allowing sunlight and a breeze to filter through the screen door. Since P.J. died, the windowless front door remained shut.

A breeze rattled the willow branches across the brittle grass. From the top of the hill, Martha could see Gina's red Camaro turn right onto the highway. Exhaust plumed from the tailpipe. The rear tires squealed. Martha's ribs tightened.

She wasn't ready to let Sandra go. Maybe Sandra wasn't ready to go.

By instinct, Martha turned toward her thinking spot, which more recently served as her crying spot. She hiked to the edge of the woods just above the church where the oaks and tulip poplars opened to a field of tall fescue and chigger weeds.

Martha sat on a scrubby patch of grass and rested her elbows on bent knees. The sun baked the tops of her ears. The hillside swelled with the sugary scent of the honeysuckle vine that wove along the barbed wire fence marking the edge of the Creekmore farm. On the road below, Martha watched a pickup whip around the tight curve, its driver emboldened by his familiarity of the route.

The cicadas' thrum muffled the rumble of eighteen-wheelers on the interstate in the distance. Ninety miles up the road. That's how far away Sandra would be at college. Martha had bought two maps of Lexington— one for herself and one for Sandra. In the blue-gray stillness of the early morning, coffee percolating on the stovetop, she studied them by lamplight at the kitchen table before anyone else stirred. She traced the streets of the downtown, ran her finger along routes through the campus, drew small stars on the cafeteria, the library, and Sandra's dormitory, only a vague idea of what these buildings must look like.

Sandra would be a college graduate with letters behind her name. Martha considered her own pedigree: Pregnant four times, mother of three. Wife of nineteen years. Loyal friend. Best chowchow canner in Wickers Bend. Expert wound dresser. Sunday school teacher. Occasional doubter of doctrine. Handyman and snake killer when Raymond took a double shift, and sometimes, even when he was home.

Years ago, she watched I-75 being built from this spot. First, the road crews leveled dirt. It took a year just to move it all. They dug and dug. Martha heard they'd found chunks of old pottery, the frame of a Model-T, and even human bones.

A few days ago, she'd dug potatoes with Miriam in her garden. They turned the dirt with hoes, then sifted through the clods for brown-skinned spuds. The damp soil caked under their nails. They worked quietly, side by side, Martha aiding her friend the only way she knew how.

Miriam had broken the silence. "The deeper you dig, the colder the ground. And so dark." She wiped the sweat from her forehead and left of smudge of dirt in its place. "P.J.'s buried underground like one of these potatoes." Her upper lip trembled and she looked across the crest of a distant hill to gain composure. "I worry he's cold."

"I know, Miriam," was all Martha knew to say.

That day in the garden, Miriam had thought about her own Mamma and Daddy. That day, she'd thought of all the snakes she'd beaten to death with the sharp of edge of the shovel blade and then buried with the very same tool. Now in her thinking spot, she thought about the sweat and blood of those I-75 road crews as well as the bones they found. Everybody and everything found its way into the dirt somehow.

In the distance, traffic rolled down I-75. After those road crews had leveled the ground, they molded concrete, foot by foot, until the gray pavement stretched from Michigan to Miami. The construction lasted a decade, and Martha had watched each step, waiting for that wide interstate out of town, not a single hairpin curve in sight, to be built. She rubbed at a sunspot on the back of her hand, as if she could wipe it off with enough friction. She wondered if Sandra, her light brown head bobbing up and down in Laurel Lake, even realized the good years those men poured into the fill of the highway that would carry her to college. Martha wondered if those men ever wanted some of those years back.

Elaine Fowler Palencia

Moving On

For generations my people have died
in a letter or in a phone call
from a distant hospital or once,
from a detective in Middletown, Ohio.
We wandered through backcountry
from France to the Low Countries
to Ireland to America,
or from Scotland to Ireland to America,
or from England to indentured Virginia.
We peeled off the Great Wagon Road
as it went south, stopping
on remote plots of land
for a few decades to clear newground,
farm, and ply a trade—
weaving, blacksmithing,
teaching, preaching, distilling—
before pushing on.
We couldn't afford to stay
or were restless for better,
venturing farther and farther
away from each other
to try our luck in post-Civil War
Missouri, Texas, and Arkansas,
or in the industrial Midwest
in tourist Florida, rural California.
Quakers and Presbyterians
became Methodists, Baptists
and Holy Rollers, suspicious
of the new, yet compelled to seek
the edges of our known world,
permanent immigrants in a country
where we have never felt quite at home
but which has given us enduring memories
of having once belonged in a place
where we could wear our own faces—
a holler with woods, a creek, a field, a barn,
a small, hillside cemetery.

Elaine Fowler Palencia

Her Work

She rocked side to side on arthritic bowlegs,
her wide hips in buttermilk-smelling wash dresses
cutting a swath through the work day
of milking, canning, freezing, cooking, mending, washing,
caring for the daughter who forgot how to walk,
yoked with an aging husband who also knew only work,
her knobbed hands cuffing biscuits into shape before dawn
and chording hymns on the old upright after dark.
She came from people who couldn't show affection,
after all, it was unseemly and forward,
but when the children and grandchildren
came to visit in summer, they found
she had put down her broom handle stick
and pulled herself up steep stairs
by means of a wooden handrail
to the unused upper floor of the old house
and there made up two ancient beds and a cot
with sun-dried sheets and blankets and somehow
must have gotten on her knees and leaned over
the edge of the bathtub to scour it, because
we found grains of cleanser around the drain.
From the newly washed window on the landing
we could look out over the whole thirty acres,
the barn, chicken coop, and fields
we saw twice a year, then once,
then now, in memory.

Elaine Fowler Palencia

Driving the River Road, Pomeroy, Ohio, to Huntington, West Virginia

the Ohio smooth as Sunday morning

on the West Virginia side
a line of low hills as even as a couch back
and behind them, farms
my family lost one way or another

deer flip up white tails
as they bound
in front of the car
clear a ditch
miss two small roadside crosses

yet another vast installation
of concrete, smokestacks, and lights,
implacable as the Death Star

tired pickup trucks
homebound at dusk

then a town:
an abandoned barbecue joint
a grade school
a clutch of houses with yard signs
Vote no on the school levy

        over which

the hunter's moon rises like a yawn

Linda Parsons

Light Around Trees in Morning

So much light, I think it's caught fire,
the paperbark maple self-immolating—
but it's only the coppery scrolls' silhouette
facing east. Someone once important
to me planted this tree, led friends to this
very spot as if it were the only blaze,
the garden's only crown.

Importance ebbs in time, keeping its own
mystery, and we're left on our knees,
in cinders, smoldering ash, as I was,
turning to what's more important—
clover in the iris, stones overrun
with chocolate mint, the scrawl
of minor serpents to read and expel.

A woman alone makes good headway
in the weeds, my corona unscrolling
like fiery swords at the entrance of nothing
and everything Edenic. Sometimes I think
light comes only when we're bowed
too low to notice our leaves and limbs
burnished by morning, our bodies
in spontaneous combustion.

Linda Parsons

Visitation: Mother

Today I barely beat the rain to cut back a wild-haired spirea, chartreuse in spring and summer with snowflake flowers—but in that spot, under a neighbor's weed tree, it always darkens with a fall fungus. I stuff the black stalks in the bin, step on lemon balm and oregano. Their scents comingle, like dinner on the grounds, like a flag raised among the wounded. Sometimes the field of our story is equally ruined. We are sometimes the leaving and sometimes the left. At eleven, I left my troubled mother for my stepmother's olive branch. Between us, a singed no man's land of attrition. When I see my mother now in the nursing home, we want to get close and touch. She marvels at my hair, the same blinding white as hers. She knows that something happened in our past but, over the blaring TV, she can't quite put her finger on it. To get to her, I walk through the waste I chopped off in light rain until my arms ached. I lean to speak in her good ear. I can't say her voice is the balm of herbs crushed underfoot, a voice that once froze me to the core. I can't say the air of bodies waiting to die doesn't make me sick, but a little peace creeps in. Along the way, I have been both the leaving and the left—the seed and the dung—both needed to till the ground and bear fruit. My mother lets herself stand in the field of some small memory of a daughter she lost. I let myself take her silky hand.

Linda Parsons

Come Home

Tonight the gloaming is a shadowbox
of corridors, time-dimmed as the Sunday
School room of ancient ladies my grandmother
called *Miss* in formality: Miss Rose Davis,
Miss Mary Holt. The ancient world mapped
those yellowed walls—Paul's travels
through Antioch in Syria, Macedonia,
Corinth. Paul the tentmaker mending
the knotted nets, converted in a flash
to a fisher of men.

Cicadas start late this summer, not yet
a blast like Paul's fiery Damascus moment—
more like my grandmother singing
from the *Broadman*, her vibrato rising
and settling around me, already asleep
in her lap. *Take me, take me, mememe,*
they rapture in high fidelity, their invitation
in the half-light: *Ye who are weary,*
come home.

Nearing seventy, my own gloaming,
I watch only for the soft tent of night
to fall. Insect voices I wait for all year
call from the canopy, primitive and unnamable.
The portals of home always lit, always open,
map where I've tripped and was pardoned
beyond reason, blasted deaf and blind
by mercy. *Take me*, I reply, *me*,
and they open wider still.

Kory Wells

The Electronics Lab, Early Eighties, or
Signal Voltage as a Function of Time

On the oldest corner of my college campus,
even then the lab was a throwback—
unairconditioned, musty, clunky metal
and wood workbenches so tall their lips
brushed my chest as I climbed
onto a stool at my station's black-topped
slate of resistance. The instructor—
it didn't matter which—walked with a certain
swagger, no matter bald spot or pot belly,
if any girls were in the room. We whispered rumors
about the good-looking one, what he'd tried
to touch as he leaned close to check a circuit.
I'd learned not to raise any question
when he walked by, although I couldn't
help but wonder how he'd kiss.

I tried not to blush at the lexicon of
male and female, strippers and poles,
to focus instead on protons, neutrons,
most of all those free-spirited electrons—
they moved and I measured,
even controlled their flow. I'd flick a switch
and watch the oscilloscope's graph change
from square wave to curvaceous sine,
prompting even the nicest boys
to thumb the knobs and adjust the curve
until anyone with hormones could see
breast after breast after perfect breast.
Oh, look, it's my girlfriend, they'd say.

Back then the only girl didn't say
that's inappropriate. She didn't say
you're making me uncomfortable.
She didn't say shut the hell up. Back then
the only girl could only try not to think
of her own 34As, try not to think anything
about her body. But somewhere inside it,
a load grew.

I was learning about power.

Kory Wells

Hounded by what used to be,

my breasts these days mope
around the house like pups
with tails between their legs,

a worn-out simile
the old dogs have earned.
Who's been a good girl?

I distract them with treats,
but they whine when I reach for
my bra. *We don't wanna*

go out on leash. They do
perk up for poetry and poker
nights, when—tipsy on smoked

bacon and bourbon—
they let go and howl: it's belly
who's really let things go.

Smack talk. Don't think for one
newton of gravity they regret
only their lost looks. A rumble

in my gut and how they whimper:
It still knows the mouth, the tongue.
They have only memories.

Those nights they worked like dogs.
Enticing lovers.
Keeping small humans alive.

Kory Wells

Tradition Is a Body

A kinship of casseroles, too many
cousins in my small kitchen, talk
slick as hot buttered rolls:
You're better-looking every time
I see you; those cookies
are calorie-free today.
Yet I miss our gatherings
of twenty years ago,
the whole house a hubbub
of aunts and uncles, children
and grands. Bodies of my body,
bodies from which I came—
changing, disappearing, you keep me
in need. Gravy can't fill every hunger.
Still, after second helpings
and old stories, we push back
from the table, groaning.
All of our bodies closer
to leaving. None of our bodies
wanting to go.

Natalie Sypolt

Blood Harmony

—excerpt from novel in progress

Prologue

Blood Harmony. In music, this term is used to reference the unique singing harmony that only blood relations can create. This cannot be taught, and is a natural and unique sound, often said to cut right to the core of the listener. This term has also been used in medicine, when doctors ask family members to come in and speak to a comatose patient. It is genetics, and this sound of a sibling or parent is the closest thing to the patient's very own voice, and the hope is that the sound will reverberate somewhere deep inside, and bring the patient back to the world.

Chapter 9

When we were little, before Daddy left, we'd sometimes go over to my grandma's house on Friday nights. It was just me and Jake because we were the oldest, and the other girls were still hanging on Mom. All my uncles would come in, fresh from work, tired and dirty and grouchy, but then someone would pull out his guitar and then all the instruments would start to appear like magic. We hadn't seen anyone carry them in, but there was a banjo and a mandolin and a fiddle. No one would guess it to know them, but Daddy's people were all musical and could pick up just about any instrument at all and play it by the end of an hour, just by feeling it and listening. My grandad and his brothers were the same way. The way he and grandma met was that they used to go around and play and sing sometimes, and once went to my grandma's school. To hear her tell it, it was love at first sight, even though she was only about eleven at the time.

They'd usually start just by tuning, and I'd sit on the floor cross legged at Daddy's feet, and Jake would be on the couch next to him. On those nights, Daddy was like a magnet and we both just kept getting closer and closer and closer.

The boys could all play but only Grandma was a very good singer on her own. Her voice had this sound like it started down in a holler then worked its way up, high into her head, in the mountains. There wasn't another sound in the world I could think of to compare it to; still can't. But I think it hurt her somehow, to sing that way, and she'd usually do just one song that had all the men wiping their eyes after, then could not be talked into doing another.

The men could all carry a tune (unlike me, who Daddy said couldn't carry a tune in a bucket), but when they hit together, it was a different kind of sound—a vibration almost that sounded so good and right, even I could tell it.

"It's the blood harmony," Grandma said once. "Like knows like, even in voices, and they just fit together."

I guess at the time I maybe thought it was just one of those things she sometimes said—like when the sun is shining and it's raining at the same time, that means the devil is beating his wife—but now I know there is truth to it, and that lots of singing groups made up of family members had this blood harmony—Carter Family, Everly Brothers, the Louvin Brothers—and that even doctors understand it, and that's why they want close family to talk to someone when they're in a coma, to try to bring them back.

When Jake got a little older, maybe 11 or 12, Daddy could see him itching to join in. He'd start moving his mouth a little when they'd sing, so Daddy told him to come on and sing if he was going to, instead of just mushing his mouth around, and he did. Just like the others, on his own, he sounded like a boy, okay but a little lonely. When Daddy joined in with him, though, it was the vibration. The blood harmony that I could feel in my belly as I listened, that raised up the hairs on my arms.

The first time it happened, Daddy and Jake both seemed breathless at the end of the song—just "Down in the Valley" which we'd all sang a million times. Jake's face was rosy and Daddy had tears in his eyes. He slapped Jake on the back, and they locked eyes for a minute. I could've felt left out, sad not to be a part of the family magic happening between them, but instead I was just mesmerized. Then the spell was quickly broken as one of my uncles started in fast on "Shady Grove." Jake looked at me, smiling so big, then slapped me hard on the back just as Daddy had slapped him.

Those nights were some of my favorites, and always started out so good, until everybody had too much to drink, would start talking more than playing, and eventually someone would hit on some old hurt and the brothers would want to fight. More often than not, Daddy was right in the middle of it, and we'd end up leaving in a huff, him stomping hard on the porch and slamming the screen door.

Jake would drive us home usually, unless Daddy's fight had sobered him up. Jake had known how to drive since he was just little, even before he could reach the pedals and steer while sitting on Daddy's lap. He'd navigate us up out of Grandma's holler and then the two or three miles on the hard road, before turning and slow going down into our holler. He was so serious, both hands tight on the wheel and never taking his eyes off the road. I remember it being so dark, late as it was, and feeling like we were the only ones in the whole world.

I didn't care a bit about singing, but I wanted to drive, and pestered Jake about letting me. "No, Tess," he'd say. "You're too little."

"I am not!" I'd always make sure I was sitting in the middle of the bench set in Daddy's truck, right next to Jake. Daddy would be slumped against the door, or sometimes would ride with his head partially out the window like a hound dog, if his drunk was a happy instead of raging one.

"You don't want to," Jake would say. "It's not fun like you think."

"Oh yeah. Right. You're just saying that because you want to be the one to do it. You always get to do everything."

I loved Jake more than anyone in the whole world, but I was his little sister, and sometimes the perfection I saw in him got damned annoying. I wanted some of that, just once.

"You think I want—" I had pushed a button just enough and made Jake just mad enough that he took his eyes off the road to glare at me. We were on the hard road, just before turning down into our place, and all of a sudden, I saw lights coming at us out of nowhere. When Jake turned to yell at me, he'd steered right into the other lane. I thought for sure we were about to die, but quicker than anything, Daddy had reached across me, grabbed the wheel, and yanked us back into our lane, just missing the other truck. Jake pushed the brakes hard, and we came to a gravel throwing stop right there. He was breathing hard and so was I. Daddy was already slumped back against the door, his hat pulled down over his eyes.

"Keep your eyes on the road," he mumbled.

Jake wanted to cry, I think, but wouldn't let himself, so I did it for him. I curled into his side, buried my face in his flannel shirt, balled it up in my fists.

"Get on home," Daddy said, never looking at us at all. Jake slowly took his foot off the brake, and we rolled forward again.

As far as I know, no one ever told Mom about what had happened, and I never asked to drive again. There weren't many more nights like that before Daddy left, started his new family. He didn't teach me to drive, or anything really, other than to keep my eyes on the road all the time.

Roberta Schultz

Starlight (Song)

Once there was a pink house on a gravel lane.
A little family lived there through pleasure and pain,
and they sat out on the clear nights to marvel at the stars,
but they're nothing but a memory now.

Once there were three sisters rambling through the woods.
They learned the names of flowers, unlearned all their shoulds,
and they climbed the low-limbed maples when their neighbor taught them how,
but they're nothing but a memory now.

CHORUS

Nothing but the kindness. The leave-it-all-behind-us.
The truth would only blind us to light.

Their parents often stumbled, as parents often do.
Mom said she was "dirty," and Daddy was "dirty-two."
And they squealed each time she said this 'cause to them all jokes were new,
but they're nothing but a memory now.

BRIDGE

Some stars up in the skies are old worlds that have died, but they shine for our eyes.
Far off glowing embers. How space-time remembers…

CHORUS

Nothing but the kindness. The leave-it-all-behind-us.
a little glint of starlight now.

Roberta Schultz

Home Brew (Song)

Toss a dash of respect into the roiling pot.
Add a pinch of your grin when the water's hot.
Have a cool glass of mercy handy and standing by.
Keep the lid on, 'cause boil-overs will happen.

Choose the grain. Choose the hops with some extra care.
Home brew should be tasty so nothing can compare.
Whip some yeast in the bucket, then snap the lid on tight.
Turn the lights out, and let the magic ferment.

CHORUS

Then, in that last step add some sugar. Nothing bubbles if you don't.
Not worth thinking, not worth drinking if you won't
take your time and add some sugar.

Make time to bottle it and label it.
Taste the goodness that you've made.
If you're lucky, you'll have brew enough for two.
So, enjoy your long drink at the table.

CHORUS (2nd ending)

Then, in that last step add some sugar. Nothing bubbles if you don't.
Not worth thinking, not worth drinking if you won't
take your time and add some sugar.

Make time to bottle it and label it.
Taste the goodness that you've made.
If you're lucky, you'll have brew enough for two.
You'll be fine, if you only add some sugar.

Tina Parker

Lee Highway

1.

Lee Highway begins in a mountain town
On a cul-de-sac above the Electrolux Plant
Follow the neighborhood of streets named
Tall Timber, Cherokee, Shawnee, and Cheyenne

To reach the starting line in Bristol on the Virginia side
Drive through the one-lane underpass curve
Around Beaver Creek to the Shoney's Big Boy
Home of the midnight breakfast buffet,
Sirloin tips, strawberry pie whole or sliced.

2.

Outside town Virginia is a row of motor court motels
The General Lee
Stardust Lodge
Rainbow Inn
Their heyday long gone since I-81 cut through

No more water in the pools
Sky blue insides scraped to white and gray
By devil worshipers or skateboarders
Which is worse

The motels went first
No tourists on this highway
Since before I was born
Suburban Shoes
Dixie Pottery
The Moonlite Drive-In
Would hold on for the rest of my youth

Not so my first best friend Misty
She lived in the mobile home park off the highway
And set further back my friends Tearsa and Dreama
Their daddy's big rig parked in the front yard

They all up and moved
To the Tennessee side before junior high.

3.

My dad's Econoline was made for the old road
It carried us down Lee Highway to Highway 52
The two-lane road that wove a ribbon
Over the mountain to West Virginia

The way my parents drove
From Bluefield to Bristol
First night newlyweds in the town
That would become home

Now they look for landmarks
Any sign of places they once knew
In the back my brother howls for food
For a drink to be anywhere but this curlicue
Road with no Golden Arches no Burger King
Not even a Dairy Queen

The van feels big as the coal trucks
The club seat an island
That holds all I need
My books and a sliding-door length window

My eyes search the kudzu that took
The company store, the church, and the UMWA
It's country roads take me home but what happens
When that home was on Shanty Hill

And I'll never see the outhouse the company paid
Caledonia and Old Folks to clean though I can hear
The screen door slam behind my aunt Poochie
As she flew out the back door and down the cement stairs
All that's left of the house to prove
It was ever there.

4.

Where does the Lee Highway end
Does it end in the cadence of a polluted creek
With a song that is the way my people speak
Does it end in misunderstood complexity
With a bad rep its secrets my history

Does it end in tragedy
My classmate on the way to a ball game
My brother's friend off to college when
Head on
Low visibility
No helmet
Crash

Let it end deep in the mountain
The only light shining from the center
Of granddaddy's hard hat
As he fixes machines down in the mines

Let it end at the picket line
Hit the bricks and say it straight
May the road make my belly
Drop make me carnival-ride scrambled
Weightless let me take flight
On these Himalaya bruise-your-thigh curves.

5.

How many times did we make the trip
Virginia to West Virginia and back
So many it makes sense that I am comfortable
On a curve don't mind not seeing what lies
Just beyond the hairpin
Cut the engine I want to climb
The rock ledge Look
                                        Out
Let me stand here and drink it in
More than mountains it is endless
Vista that is mystery is memory is always
Out of reach even as I open
My arms wide and plead for more.

Tina Parker

For My Mountain Uncles, Those Men Long Gone

You rose from coal dust
Played ball on the slate pile
Your feet splashed red
Clouded creek water.

You smelled of cigarettes
Red Man and Jim Beam
You were all limbs
Long arms that wrapped
Me tight, hung easy
On the porch swing.

I never saw you angry
Not once
Though your people
Started famous feuds
And your hollers
Echoed gunfire.

I would honor you
But I've no boys
To take your names
No boys
To raise up right.

I would teach them
To open the door
Ladies first
To take their hats
Off in church.

My girls won't know
Men like you.
They will need
To treat themselves
Fine, to walk tall
Like they are meant
To be first.

They will need
Pistols tucked in
Shiny black purses

And handkerchiefs
That are always clean.

Tina Parker

One Thanksgiving I Made a General Jackson Pie

That's what my Nanny called
A chocolate pecan pie
But how long would it bake
I was in a different state
And asked her over the phone
As I yanked the oven door
Open again
      Has it set yet
      It needs to set
But how will I know
How can I tell it's done

Her soap operas blared
Through the phone
Nanny . . . Nanny?
I wish you were here to eat
A piece with me
Her voice a whisper
Through the static
      I love you Tina girl
And she was gone.

Karen Whittington Nelson

Downriver

Even at its most wicked, this stretch of the Licking River has more in common with a sulking child than a rampaging bully. Now with summer's drought, it's a lazy garter snake slithering through the valley past corn fields, fishing shacks, rusted trailers with tarpaulin roofs and outhouses concealed by willow trees.

Just above Dillon Bridge, the water runs languid and trickles over golden shale. Great Blue Herons stand midriver in inches-deep water, spear hapless fish floundering in the shallows. When startled, the birds express their annoyance with a single squawk before carrying the memory of water skyward on slowly undulating gray wings that break like waves against parched clouds.

A rock's throw downriver of the bridge, a great boulder slab juts from the tangled shore and snags the deepest currents. My mother claims this boulder, swears her initials carved into the rock give proof of ownership as good as any bureaucrat's rubber-stamped gibberish. She sits upon the flat rock in a webbed lawn chair reading a book. The scent of her sunbaked skin is delicious. Steamy, baby oil ghosts and perspiration blend, shimmer and dance above her smooth arms and legs before disappearing.

My sister and I wear bathing suits wet and itchy with grit. We lie on our stomachs over bath towels worn so thin that our skinny hip bones and knobby knees are chafed by the rock. Our torsos are propped up on calloused elbows; our heads swivel in our palms and follow the sun. Squinting behind dime store sunglasses we tell knock-knock jokes and watch piss ants make off with the crumbs of our peanut butter and jelly sandwiches.

We're anxious as otter kits to shimmy back down the ledge into the water, but Mom insists that we rest and wait for our picnic lunches to digest. Sis sulks, grows whiny and eventually begins to nod. I fend off sleepiness, creep on my belly across the rockface and press an ear to the gritty coolness of the crumbling edge. I begin counting the minutes left until our mother will release us, "One Mississippi, two Mississippi..." Five feet below my head, I sense the river slowing, exploring, tasting the rock with her prying tongue. I hear her fluid voice, smooth as the tumbled-glass shard held curled in my palm; the melody, tinged blue-green, dances like the sun spots beneath my eyelids. The river sings to her silver-scaled children and me, of timeless mysteries lurking beneath the great rock's underbelly....

As if from a far-away place, I hear a child's scream mimicking my own middle-of-the-night voice, "Do you feel it? We're moving!"

My sister's eyes pop. She jumps up, scrambles toward the rock's edge. Mom springs from her chair. It collapses and skids across the rock. The baby oil bottle tips and the glistening goo puddles in a pockmarked depression. Mom grabs my sister by a swim-suit ruffle, pulls her back, plops her down on her towel. She turns to me with wild eyes and yells, "Stop teasing! And for the love of Mike, sit down!"

"I'm sorry," I mumble, and sink into the gritty, sticky puddle. But I'm not sorry; I'm mad, shaking. I want to scream at my mother, insist that we are moving—the water, the rock, the sun. The fish, the birds, the clouds, the minutes, everything—moving on. I want to cry, climb onto her lap and whisper in her ear, "How long have you known?" I want to cling to her, to be rocked and reassured. Instead, I fake remorse, pull my towel over my head and turn away from my mother, until she releases us, back into the river.

I had so wanted to tell her that I knew what I knew, but I hadn't the words to make my argument. I didn't yet know that anything I may have said then, or since, would only have been redundant.

Bonnie Proudfoot

Holding On

We bought a crooked house
on a rolling knob
a jagged diagonal slice
of a partly wooded hilltop
a hand-dug basement and
screened-in porch,
sloping floors, un-square
rooms, walls stuffed
with faded newspapers,
yesterday's weather,
ads, and squabbles.
Slate slabs hauled
from the creek,
once formed a path,
now they sink and
crumble. Outside is
always in, pebbles stick
to boot treads and mud
to pant knees, fingernails.
Windows and doors can't be
coaxed to close, even new
ones shift shape. Us too,
our bodies tethered
by twisted threads, the hills
and valleys of us, all
falling out of line and
falling back into it,
holding on to less each day.

Bonnie Proudfoot

Lessons

—after Limon's "The First Lesson"

She placed the boneless breast
between two pieces
of wax paper, pounded it with the points

of a meat mallet, squat flesh resisting
as if alive,
then meat beginning to spread

wider, longer, shape breaking down.
This is how
you soften it, she said. She wasn't afraid

to use force. When her fingers curled
and calcified,
and she could no longer slap my cheek

with a swift hand, she took a hairbrush
to me for backtalk,
but I did not get softer. I got tough.

And when a wildness came over my son,
I remember
pulling back my arm, then stopping.

The world is already too tough.
He needed to be
tender to learn this for himself.

Cathy Cultice Lentes

Chillicothe

...comes from the Shawnee Cha-la-gaw-tha.
The Shawnee people used this term as a name for the settlement
that was home to their principal leader—
as Chillicothe literally means "principal town."

Where hills ended, and plains began,
she could breathe again, lungs opening, closing
like bellows pumping air in and out, as the low

fire of sunset burned a path toward home: the welcoming
oaks and hickory of her childhood yard, neighboring fields
of wheat and corn, and the surety of a horizon for direction.

Returned to that landscape, she remembered the girl who read
the rough braille of bark, inhaled the sharp secrets of acorns,
and witched mud potions in a spiked cauldron of stump.

For years, she believed it was the hills of her new home
that smothered her, squeezed her mind dim and hard, but when
he left, bad air cleared the sky.

Now when she crosses, driving east or west, the Scioto sings to her
differently: Chillicothe as portal. Chillicothe as bridge, two halves
of one self, flowing, her principal power residing within.

Laura Leigh Morris

Monster

When the ultrasound tech went quiet, she grabbed her husband's hand. When the tech spoke again in a much higher voice, she could barely breathe. She could only shake her head when they asked if she wanted to know the baby's sex. By the time the obstetrician entered the room, she was convinced the baby would die. So when he said, "The baby has some concerning growths," she said, "Thank god," even though she didn't know how concerned she should be.

The doctor and tech both kept their faces neutral as images flashed on the screen. "As you can see, the baby's body looks healthy—the organs are developing on schedule, the legs and arms are measuring just where we want them at 20 weeks. All good news." His voice grew softer when he said, "There are a couple of abnormalities you need to be aware of." He switched to a facial view of her baby. The giant orbs where its eyes were made it look like an alien, but that's not where he gestured. Instead, he pointed to the skull itself. "As you can see, there are a number of bony protrusions." He ran the cursor over lumps on the baby's head. "The interior of the skull looks perfect, and the baby's brain appears to be developing normally. The exterior of the skull is what gives us pause."

Her husband gave her hand a reassuring squeeze, but the knot in her stomach wouldn't let loose. She'd been dreaming of this moment for weeks, planning to share the ultrasound pictures in her announcement. Her friend had photoshopped a pink bow on the baby's head in hers. But she couldn't send this—Surprise! We're having a potato!

"The buildup of bone is especially dense here and here." He highlighted two spots on either side of the baby's forehead. Now, it looked like an alien with horns. Surprise! We're having a water buffalo!

He opened another image, but she couldn't decipher what part of the body they were looking at. "Here's the other area you should be aware of."

She noticed how neutral he kept his language, how he seemed to be trying not to frighten them. It was clearly working on her husband, who smiled and nodded, anxious to please.

The doctor pointed to something that looked like a snake. "We call this a vestigial tail. Normally, it disappears around the eighth week of gestation, becoming the coccyx, but in this case it looks like your baby might be born with it." He turned to them. "Now, a vestigial tail is rare but not unheard of. And after the baby is born, as long as it doesn't contain any spinal tissue, we can remove it with a quick surgery. Still, your baby's tail is longer than I've seen before."

"So you've dealt with this?" her husband asked. Like baby tails were common conversation.

Ever since two lines had appeared on the stick, she'd been picking out nursery furniture, planning colors, buying clothes. No way those cute onesies had room for a tail. The tiny hats would have no space for horns. Surprise! We're having a freak!

"No." The doctor drew the word out, rubbed his chin. "I've read about it."

Not good enough, she wanted to say but couldn't unstick her tongue from the top of her mouth.

"The bony protrusions along with the tail tell me there's something we're not seeing, something we don't know yet." The doctor was measuring his words. Her husband kept nodding. She bit her lip. Hard. Tasted blood. "I'm sending you to a specialist, a doctor who can get the answers we need." He leaned forward, touched the back of her hand. She flinched. Mother to a beast. "I won't tell you not to worry, but don't worry too much. We don't know anything yet. For all we know, your baby could have a bumpy head and a little scar on their backside."

Surprise! Only half a monster!

***

Her husband prattled on while she dressed, but she heard nothing. He held his phone toward her, said, "I've already found three support groups." She turned away, wanted to slap the phone from his hand. He kept talking as she followed him through the hallways, down the elevator, across the lot, and to the car. That false cheer in his voice, the tone he used in his first grade classroom.

Once they were both buckled in, he turned to her. "Don't you have anything to say?"

Since the test came up positive, she'd been picturing this baby—his blonde hair, her blue eyes, rosebud lips. A baby made for Gerber commercials. Matching outfits in their family pictures.

"Anything at all?" her husband asked.

She shook her head. Her baby. With horns. A tail. Her sweet, sweet baby. Surprise! A wildebeest!

Her husband sighed, put the car in gear, exited the lot. He turned on the radio, but she switched it off, couldn't stand the noise. The only sound was the rumble of tires on the road, other cars' motors, occasional honks.

"The baby could be fine," he said.

The silence dragged out.

Then, a waver in his voice, "I'm scared too."

She breathed deeper, felt their fear mingle. The car was filled with it. She cracked the window. He was biting his lip, his chin quivering, on the verge of tears.

"The baby looks like a devil," she whispered.

"We could call him Beelzebub. Bub for short."

"That's not funny." Though it kind of was.

"Lucifer. Call her Lucy," he said.

She cracked a smile for the first time.

"Damien for a boy," he added and put his hand on her stomach.

She put her hand over his, pressed. "Lilith for a girl."

Catherine Carter

My mother's recipe leaves out ingredients

for her cider-sweet apple cake, last
relic of a lost friend. Her list
omits the apples—what kind, how many,
whether to peel—leaves out the scatter
of slices between pours of batter,
leaves out the heat and how long to bake;
in her fine hand, *orange juice* reads
rage giver. She's like the careful witch
whose spells skip every second step,
omit the key word of the chant so
only the initiate know, maybe
because she knows some things can only
be transmitted by breath, friend to friend,
mother to daughter, the end words
of those gone, or going, too soon.
So I can't make this cake unless she's there
to explicate the hidden spices,
the unwritten pieces; and so I
have to come home each time to learn
again, both that and other things,
lest that bespattered card should take
her cake too back into the earth
beneath a dark moon, when she turns
to follow all the apples where they go.

Catherine Carter

During the long meeting things begin to change:

scowl lines and smile lines slowly become grooves,
then gullies into which wild horses could wander
like canyon mazes and die there, unable to find
water or the way out, and the oblong yellow notepad
on the conference table reveals itself to be a trap-
door, the kind laid in old houses' kitchen
floors. It lifts into one stealthy hand
with a quiet hinge-cry; she steps
softly to the seat of her chair and then
to the tabletop and then down the unpainted,
unrailed plank stairs into the cool
smells of dog hair, stone and the soundless
water that seeps from stone. The light is a faint
gray gleam from a dusty ground-level pane,
catching briefly in canning jars filmed with grime.
Startled by shift and creak, a brown wolf
spider, palm-sized, pauses to stare, then flicks
away at the renewed voice-rumble overhead.
In the twilight she can see
the foundations, the underpinnings
of everything. The pillars bearing the ceiling-
joists were once small trees, cut trunks sanded
something like smooth, firmer than cement, shielded
from weather and rot. A hundred years
and more, they have held up what's overhead,
and now, steady and hard, they hold
even more: the budget on the table, the hissing
heating ducts, the freight and weight
of administrative hierarchy, the oblivious
committee setting deadlines, earnestly debating dates
while, underground, she stoops
to the limewashed floor to take up a round gold
rutabaga, still unshriveled, which someone before
her must have left or forgotten here: a token
of faith or warning, a word in code, a sign.

Catherine Carter

Till the cows come home

I have been waiting a decade
and more, standing out in this now-
autumn pasture—same lightning-struck sassafras
standing warped and riven afternoon
after morning, winter after fall,
same tawny broomsedge feathering
seedpuffs into the wind—
straining for the distant clank
of cowbells. As evening lengthens
I tell myself the splotched shadow
under the far pine is a Holstein, black
paintsplash over dingy flanks,
that clump of broomsedge is a fawn
Jersey, dropping her wide ears to pull
fescue, and that burnt stump is a black
Angus calf, irritably switching his tail,
and that although they don't want me to know,
they are all ambling peaceably
toward me and toward the barn beyond,
though the east end of its roof
has fallen in and no clover
or alfalfa has sweetened its rotting
loft all the years I've stood here
waiting. Surely I see them now.
I can wait forever for cows,
as they waited once for their lowing calves
to be returned from the heavy trucks.
I can see anything, believe anything,
except that what will never
come again will in fact never come
again, that Bossy and Buttercup
and Bess are long gone to feedlot
and slaughterhouse, conveyor-
belt and hammerstroke, that neither you
nor those cows is ever coming home.

Lisa J. Parker

Gather

—Hindman Settlement School, Kentucky, April 2023

Night rain gathers the slick-slip
of pollen-dusted leaves, drops
sleepy greens of white pine,
black locust, and maple into
the meandering stream-fall.

I wake to boisterous blue jays,
watch from porch front the quiet work
of robins who pull worm after
worm, hopping one spot of soaked ground
to the next, their muted pleasure
a sustained note beneath the call
and answer of cardinal pairs,
scratch of chickadee feet grabbing
honeysuckle vine wrapped from ground
to tip of hulking sycamores
that bend over falling creek
where chipping sparrows guard the shores
as each one hops in the cold branch,
throws a spray against chest and back,
flurry of wings and dipping heads.

I pull a string from my sweatshirt
drop to porch floor, watch it hang
on nails raised above cracked gray paint,
blow out to grass and ground,
maybe snatched by nest-builders,
maybe wound with moss and field grass.
I think of my old people who
buried their shed hair, a mountain
superstition about going crazy
if birds made nest or roost of those
cast-off strands, as if something
dark could come from the bits of us
woven with careful beaks into
all the soft and loamy things
that prepare a space for the new,
that cup and warm the featherless,
a piece of that home meant to be left,
to be fledged from or returned to.

Lisa J. Parker

Conviction

—In Memory of Loretta Lynn

Rattle and slide of cast iron over burners,
small black radio perched on the windowsill,
WAMU's "Stained Glass Bluegrass"
competes with clatter and racket
as grandchildren descend on the kitchen.
Grandma pours sawmill gravy two-handed
from skillet to bowl, peers over the top
of steamed glasses as she hustles plates
of salmon cakes, tomatoes, and biscuits,
kisses bedheads as she drops knives and spoons
into butter and blackstrap, and moves the radio
from sill to hutch beside the table before
Granddaddy can ask her to, and he winks at her,
pours coffee from his cup to the saucer beneath,
blows a wheezy breath across it
before he sips.

He holds his hand up over the din
to quiet us, leans his chair on back legs,
turns the knob on the radio with a grin
and "Old Camp Meetin Time" fills the room,
Loretta Lynn's unapologetic *he-yar* as she belts
I like to hear that preachin, prayin, singin, shoutin!
that driving guitar and tambourine like a tent revival.
He points a fork at us during the bridge, *That right there!*
Loretty's a downhome girl.
He sang before the Black Lung took his breath
but that was long before this table of grandchildren,
before they left hills and coalmines for valley and steel.
She hums and he taps his feet to strings and chords,
both of them paused over their plates.
I hear their dialect, their accent,
so different from my own, drift from that radio
and hold them suspended, their heads nodding,
eyes closed for those few minutes,
an altar call to the hollers they still conjure
around these plates of food, their children's children
learning how to listen.

Lisa J. Parker

Stalk: Pandemic Months

—March, 2021

I sit on the screened in porch,
listen to windchimes covered
in KN95 masks that soak
the UV light we're told will kill
whatever might still cling to them.
Every breeze twists the white cones,
hanging by earstraps, the brass chimes
clanging clumsy and entangled.

A goshawk sits on a high branch
of the winged elm we shook ice from
just a few weeks ago, the yard
still strewn with unsavable limbs
scattered across dried leaves.

I've lined the hickories and oaks
with suet baskets stuffed with granola
and berries, peanut butter and sunflowers.
The juncos and sparrows are agile
and quick, popping up into air
with any rustle or large breeze, settling
again to seeds in the grass,
but the mourning doves are cumbersome,
all flurry of cooing sounds and wings flapping
like they've never been used.

The hawk descends
and returns to its limb,
its talons empty.
Azalea bushes lining the porch
bounce and rattle
with juncos and wrens
who titter softly and share branches,
too smart to take eyes off that shadow
that moves between limb and lawn.

Meredith Sue Willis

An Old Lady of Her Own

Chapter 4: Thirteen-year-old Jenna, is about to leave her mother's apartment in a small city on the Ohio River to go live with her father and his new family in fictional Hawkinsville, West Virginia.

I put the plates in the sink, and my mother Deb got out the little dessert bowls and the ice cream. It was chocolate-chocolate chip, even though I like mocha chip better. She scooped it out, and mine had a gritty look. I pushed the bowl a few inches away.

I said, "You should have let me go to the funeral to say goodbye to Lizzie. You had no right to stop me just because you hated funerals when you were little."

She tightened up her mouth. "Funerals aren't for kids. It doesn't matter what I say, though, does it? Jenna always does what she wants, doesn't she? You watch out, Ron, she'll be running your lives before you know what hit you."

He stirred his ice cream like he wanted it to soften. "Nobody pushes Dawn around." Dawn was his new wife who I had met but didn't really know. Mostly she had seemed pretty quiet.

Bitterly, Deb said, "The only woman *you* could push around was me."

I was hoping he'd get mad and stand up and we'd storm off, but Ron just kept stirring his ice cream. When he finally ate some, I tasted mine too, and it was better than it looked, but I still didn't want it.

She put another scoop in his bowl without asking.

I said, "I'm ready to go."

They both ignored me.

"You know she has to be back over here in time for school. And she has a doctor check up. I don't want some Hawkinsville GP tending to her bruised tibia."

My bruised tibia, which I got sliding into second in softball, had ruined my whole summer. It was like if that hadn't happened, Lizzie would still be alive.

Ron said, "We have a medical center."

"Oh I'm sure you have everything a person could want over in *Hawkinsville*."

I said, "Maybe I'll see if they have a good softball team. and I'll sign up for school over there and not come back at all."

Ron finally stood up. "We'll talk next week."

I got up too. "Well call you."

I could hear her voice beginning to rev up in her throat. She was about to get hysterical. She said, "The two of you are just alike! If things don't go your way, you just walk out!"

He stopped, but kept his face turned away. "Not true, Deb."

"Which part? That when the going gets tough, you light out for the hills?"

I just wanted out of there. At the same time, part of me wanted to see a good fight.

He was looking down and speaking softly. "You're right. I shouldn't have run off. I was a kid, Deb. We were both kids."

"Oh, an apology!" cried Deb. "That's easy. Easy to say now! You got to run away and I couldn't. Someone had to take care of Jenna."

I said, "Well now you don't have to!" I went toward the door to pick up my suitcase, but I saw Lizzie's cat Bella, and picked her up instead.

Deb said, "You ran off and disappeared for years—"

"I always sent money."

"Oh yeah, ten dollars in an envelope."

Bella didn't want to be carried. I had to use two arms to hold her.

"When I was in the service—" he started.

"And now you've got a new family and you're all responsible and settled and you decide you want Jenna too!"

I said, "Stop yelling you're scaring the cat!"

Ron picked up the suitcase, the backpack, and the sack with Bella's things and went out. He didn't even say thanks for dinner.

Deb was yelling, "Go! Go ahead and Go!"

Bella tried to climb up on my shoulder, but I pressed her against my chest. We followed Ron down the stairs and out to his new truck.

He shoved mine and Bella's stuff into the second seat behind the regular seat. Deb was still yelling. She wouldn't have yelled like that if Lizzie was alive. Lizzie would have come out and said Settle Down, children. If Lizzie hadn't of died, I wouldn't have left anyhow.

I climbed up into the cab, which wasn't easy with Bella twisting around. Ron slammed my door and went to his side. The engine growled, and I knew he was about to peel out because he was so mad, but Deb was yelling,"Wait! Wait! I have something to give Jenna !"

I rolled down my window a little. "The cat's trying to get out," I said.

"I have to give you something." She pressed her fist into the space I'd left. "Take them," she said.

It was her grandmother's yellowy old imitation pearls. That was my great-grandmother. Deb used to call her affectionately Grandma Jezebel because Deb's super-religious family didn't approve of her.

"I want you to have them," said Deb. "She gave them to me."

I said, "The Jezebel pearls." Deb used to let me borrow them when I played dress up. I said, "Thank you." I hadn't hugged her good-bye.

Nobody said anything for a few seconds, then Deb said, "You have to be back for school, Jenna. I mean it, Ron. I do not give permission for her to live up there permanently."

One of the best things about Ron is that he is good at keeping quiet. He put the truck in gear and pulled away from the curb. Fast, but not too fast, not so angry anymore.

I wasn't either. I waved at Deb.

Once we were out of town and driving east, Bella settled down and then Ron started one of his speeches. When he talks, he talks all at once, in long paragraphs. He told me about the truck first, which he bought second hand. It had less than 10,000 miles on it. It was old, he said, and it had needed a good tune-up, but the paint was perfect, and the 2012's last forever. It was the fancy package, XLT 4 x 4.

Then he switched to telling me about the house in Hawkinsville, and how happy my little half-sibs were that I was coming, and how the room he was building for me was almost done, but it still had a curtain for a door, but he'd fix that soon, and Dawn had bought brand new sheets for me.

"What color sheets?"

He thought about it and said, "Blue? Or maybe kind of purple?"

I wanted to see the kids, of course, Dawn not so much. But mainly I wished we could have just kept driving like that forever, me and Ron, talking in the dark. But it was only an hour and a half. Even so, Hawkinsville was completely dead. Even the gas station was closed. Ron turned right at the only stoplight in town and geared down to climb a super steep hill that had houses, but their house was all by itself at the end of the road. It was the absolute last house in Hawkinsville with nothing but a black hill behind it.

"That's what I like," he said as we drifted into the parking area and he turned off the engine. "You have neighbors, but they aren't looking in your windows. It was her parents' house, and Dawn inherited it."

"It's your house too, isn't it?"

"It's in Dawn's name," he said.

The porch light came on.

"Well," he said, "Let's go in." It was like he wasn't in such a big hurry either. He took all my stuff again, because Bella had started to tense up.

"It's okay, Bella," I whispered. "It'll be okay."

Then an enormous dog got up off a rug in front of the door, and Bella's claws went right into my shoulder.

"Stay, Sonny," said Ron.

The dog had a big long face and floppy ears, and I could hear its tail beating on the porch boards, so it was friendly, but it didn't stay. It pressed its nose against me and tried to snuffle Bella, who was in a panic, and I had an image in my mind of her leaping out into the darkness and never coming back.

"Get away, Sonny," said Ron, giving the dog a shove. "We call him Sonny because his mother was our hunting dog, and he was the only pup of hers we ever kept."

Sonny's nose was up under Bella's tail, and Bella was hissing and scrabbling and scratching.

Ron shoved the dog away. "I mean it Sonny, leave the damn cat alone."

The door opened, and I sort of burst inside, right past Dawn. Ron came in, and Dawn closed the door. Sonny whimpered outside. For a moment we were all sort of paralyzed there, Bella's claws in my shoulder, Ron not putting the bags down, and Dawn in a thin little nightgown with puffy sleeves, holding her arms across her chest like she was cold but I think she was mad. She was shorter than me with longish medium colored hair and a smooth face that didn't show anything.

She was staring at Bella..

I said what I had prepared hours ago. "Thank you so much for letting me come, Dawn."

"Hey," said Ron, "Jenna doesn't have to say thank you, does she, Dawn? She's *home*."

Dawn said, "What's that?"

"Bella."

Ron said, "Jenna had this lady who was like her grandmother, and she died and, you know, left the cat to Jenna."

"Where does it go?" Dawn asked.

"I guess in Jenna's room—"

But I knew what she meant. I said, "There's a litter box in that sack. It'll be in the room with me."

Dawn's face was so still that suddenly I missed Deb waving her arms and doing the roller coaster voices. At least with Deb you could tell what was going on.

Finally Dawn started to move. She passed me and left the kitchen, and we followed her.

She said,"The bed's made up, and there are towels. The bathroom is between the extension and the rest of the house, so it's convenient for everybody."

"I'm going to put in a second bathroom," said Ron." At least a half bath. You wait, this place is going to be Trump Towers before we're done."

I had to say my room was big. It seemed to be my bedroom and a store room too. It had raw rafters and unfinished walls and lots of boxes. But there was a double bed and a recycled bureau painted blue, and the bed sheets and quilts were one set, a lavender and blue abstract flower pattern. There were blue towels on the bed, and Ron dumped my suitcase and backpack on the bed too. Bella seemed to be settling down, so I put her on the floor, and she went straight to Dawn and rubbed her ankles.

Dawn pushed her away.

Ron was too cheerful. "That's cats for you," he said. "They go straight for the one who doesn't like them."

"I don't have anything in particular against cats," said Dawn.

Which made me wonder if she *did* have something against teen-age step-daughters.

Sara Henning

Ash Tree (2017)

—Memorial Park, Madison, South Dakota

As a young bride I watched them, dragonflies chewing mosquitos, their mandibles gnashing wings into glass-like shards. It was summer when bluets baited the hem of my wedding dress, summer when I fantasized about jumping the Sioux quartzite bridge, trusting the rogue tenderness of water. I imagine the god of this place carrying my drowned body through fields the way, manic, I leapt from my new husband's car, threw myself into a ditch during a lightning storm, too haunted by my mother's death to go on. *Intoxicating*—that's what I called electrons zagging, the storm's return stroke rupturing the sky. I did not understand the chemistry of lightning. I did not know that memory, like grief, writes its own myth. The god of this place must be Hesiod's, not mine: nymph of the ash tree, exquisite *Melie*. In the beginning, blood drops from Uranus sculpted her spine unfurling, vertebrae like red jasper rosary beads. Her belly twists like a knife into xylem, breasts thick as pruning wounds, helicopter seeds lacing themselves into her scalp. The god of this place must be a woman, roots glittering her legs like fire agate thigh chains. Why else would algae bloom such an iridescent Pangea, dragonflies hunting the edges of a new world? I like to imagine that the god of this place carries a piece of her mother inside of her, which is why I still come here for ash trees, the scientific name of their helicopter seeds: *samara*, so much like *samsara*. They dervish through air, tiny tornadoes, dragonflies jeweling the gazebo's spindle rails. When I dream of her, the bride I was, how she drowned herself in every rogue tenderness, I thrash like bluets into the earth. The sun writes its myth on my body. I ask the god of this place to bury her like I buried my mother.

Sara Henning

Radiant Wounds (2008)

What do you call hot lavender Redbuds bleeding at interstate's edge, first seekers in a winter-killed forest? This spring, even yearning is a transplant—Redbuds, the skeletal Silver Maples so expert at playing dead. Everywhere, sepals are ready to flare. I came to Louisville not to case the Ohio river, its coal barges chuffing through mud-muscled water, not to sip Old Forester as if its oak-charred smoke in my throat was the man who once groomed me here, my body a Doc Watson cover rasping its thrall— *Summertime and the living is easy.* Summers, he slid through me like liquid blue notes—*Fish are jumping and the cotton is high.* What is pleasure when I taste him in the Hot Browns I eat with my husband now? Once, I savored tomatoes, those sliced moons, held them up to the light. Now, I bite their radiant wounds. What is pleasure when I sip an Old Fashioned, orange wheels flashing at the bottom of my rocks glass, just to stab the Luxardo cherry with my cocktail straw, bruise the heart of something sweet? I'm here for the young woman I'll never be again, the one praying over the Osage Orange tree born from a lightning bolt near Central Park. I'm here for the wine-wasted woman in Slugger Field, his hand on her thigh, bats cracking as popcorn singes the air. Would I know her now, woman who would have given him anything? *I gave him everything.* Now, hot lavender bleeds at interstate's edge. Silver Maples rush my window, ghosts of sepals sugared with snow. In another version of this story, I'm touring Millionaires Row on South Third Street, listening for yearning, stories that begin and end with a woman already dead.

Sara Henning

The Etymology of Water (2023)

When Governor Justice declares a state of emergency, I discover a whole
world deep in the belly of my house. Linoleum lifts free with the rhythm
of the flood and under, yellow epoxy gleams its cracked tempura. Century-
old turquoise calls me to its river. As generations of paint layers rise, fleck
into rhomboid silhouettes, in the naked cement, I see the shape of West
Virginia, Allegheny Mountains like a Devil's horn haunting the Eastern
panhandle. Scientists call it efflorescence, when water dissolves concrete's
alkali, when crystals rise under paint. *The resurrection of a ghost*, I think,
as water backflows from the sawed-off municipal pipe gaping from my
laundry room wall. I am shin-deep in water. My husband Shop-vacs a
slurry of dirt, the machine's guts roiling like the Mud River. My job—to
heave buckets up our basement steps to bail into the street. Rain beats my
body cold and I'm twelve again, Key West, clutched up by rip currents I
believed couldn't whisk me from the swash zone. Then, I feared nothing—
not my grandmother's salad prawns, their stare as if the dead could wake,
how she guillotined their heads with a fillet knife, slid her lacquered
fingernails under shell to rip the carapace and claws. Not my aunt, drunk
on sun and iced rosè. No one taught me to float until my body warmed at
the scrim of the Florida straits, 90 miles from Cuba, to yell until my voice
rose over the gulls and a lifeguard runs. No one came. Before the
adrenaline, before I tore through spume, the beach face my mirage of
safety, I learned any water will take the shape of the body which holds it.
Deep in the belly of my house, something is drowning. Something is being
born. In the concrete I see my new home state, gashes that could pass for
the Monongahela. I'll step over every dark thing until I believe I can carry
it—water sluicing from my hands, ghosts leaving crystals as they float to
the surface, writing their names on my skin.

Leigh Claire Schmidli

Small Hungers

Summer brought fruit. Riper, sweeter. Cheaper than any other season. And Ma bought all she could. Mangoes, rosy and plump. Berries in blue. Kiwis that she held in her hands, spooning the green flesh from its furry skin. Any piece with a thick rind, she showed how to smell at one end, a dab of sweetness there. Like perfume at a pulse.

Summer prices let the money go further and the fruits piled up in bowls throughout the kitchen, their bright colors a welcome sight after the slow spring, all that gray and damp. Their taste? A hint of what lay beyond that farm country—beyond the numbness of frost, of white skies and the workday trudging, her heels clicking steady as she cashed meager checks for weathered hands and prayed with them to the god of soft earth, the goddess of thaw. Nights, she cooked what she could, the easy and near things. The five-for-a-dollar things. Starchy browns and beige, the tired green of tinned beans. All the spice and seasoning just specks—tiny and dry.

But then came July.

It brought fruit. And light—so many hours of it—the sun sizzling through the kitchen window as it set. It brought nights when heat and humidity took over the house, making our hungers seem small. On these nights, all the curtains drawn, no lamps on, just a line of sun seeped in, maybe a breeze, and after work, Ma headed straight for her room. She traded her skirt and hose for a pair of cut-off jeans, the denim soft and loose. A token from times-had—way before she had me.

As in *Boy, we sure had some times.*

She would sway her hips then, as if she heard music—some old R&B—and with a smile, she left it at that. A piece of herself she'd keep. For herself. For those who might've known her as something else. Like, something other than Ma'am. Something other than Ma. Like, *Boy you're something else*, they might've said and they'd shorten her name to *Jo*. They'd know the perfume dabbed behind her ear and the words to those songs that made her sway.

Maybe she could hear those voices, even now, as she looked in the mirror. As she twisted and turned, taking in her curves, and I watched from the bed, reflected behind her. Another twist—and she smoothed the denim at her hips with tender hands. Another turn—and suddenly she saw me there, as if I'd just arrived. *Did you know,* she'd say, *that the core of a pineapple is called the heart?* and sauntering to the kitchen barefoot, she would tie her blouse at her midriff, roll up the sleeves and start. The sugar scent grew with every slice.

The room like dusk, the air heavy.

We leaned against the counter eating a dinner of pineapple and wedges of melon. We perched hands below mouths, let the juice fall. Drops escaped down her wrist, blotting the sleeve of her blouse. Stains like watercolors. She wouldn't notice. Leaning there, she sighed. Her bare belly showing every breath.

The oven stayed cool, dark. The pots stayed clean, the counters empty, but for a few spots of juice. Pale yellow and orange. A pool of pink. There would be no sweeping and wiping, no sink full of dishwater pruning her hands. She sighed for this rare night, the open hours. Maybe she would go down to the basement chill, uncover the old turntable and flop on the couch, playing albums she could sing to. Maybe she'd take her book down there, the love story she could never finish, her head too heavy at night—falling asleep in chairs, book open against her chest. Perhaps tonight she could get to the core of it.

Or maybe, more likely, she would go out to the yard, where the air could move. The evening sun, softer now—surely she would soak it up like a creature free of hibernation. The heat on her legs, she'd sprawl on a blanket. Holding one more palmful of mango, waiting for the sky to change and match it.

Jennifer Schomburg Kanke

They'd Arrest You for That Now

—1936

Triumph or disaster the same to them, something to do in the season
after the haying was done but before the seeds were put in.
Elsie, the driver, would let them all tie their wood sleds to the back of his
bumper. He flung the wild boys from one side of the street to the other.
Grins on their faces and snow in their boots as the onlookers hooted and
hollered, they were towheaded kings of Main Street, adrenaline junkies
nothing to lose but an afternoon and their lives, which they thought a fair
    trade for a
moment of stardom, a flash of bright steel as they flew through the town.
But at the front of the bus there was one girl who paid them no mind, she
sat
talking at length to the boy from the county home. No parents, no future,
past forgotten. Her father would flip his respectable lid if he
knew about this, if he knew of the way her mind whirled when the boy
    mentioned
anything found in the Song of Songs, especially lilies among the thorns,
especially bosoms and lips and bosoms and lips and (Oh!) lips.

Barbara Marie Minney

Queer In The Holler

She hugged a pig   rode a calf   reverse cowgirl style   cow shit gooey
on her bare feet   hills resonating with laughter   when she landed butt
first   in Steer Crick   crawdads tickling her toes   she was a boy then
queerness buried deeper than our people   on graveyard hill

He was called to *le petite mort*   boy and girl spinning together   in the
charade of mountain gods and goblins   shackled by the cognitive
disjunction of shallow rooted white pines   alcoholic sky both mask and
mirror

Mommy and daddy   never learned how to do it any other way   familiar
and unfamiliar   like clashing currents   rat snakes slithering in the air
never settling on solid soil   good memories   a twisted ball of twine

We stroll over unmarked graves daily   souls smoldering in voiceless
methanol flames   puzzle pieces the same shape and color   faces no
longer recognizable   she walks serenely out of a charnel house
covered in his blood and guts

Valerie Nieman

Wallow

Crawling into bed with yellow paint streaked
down my arm, the way I sometimes tumble
into sleep with pool water stiffening my hair
or sweat from yard work crusting to salt.

Midday Yellow, says the label, but it could be
Lemon Pie or Fuzzy Duckling or Cloudless
Sulphur Butterflies (showing themselves
at last, in October). A catalog of longing.

I don't know, I could have cleaned myself up
at least as well as my frazzled brushes, but
it's late, the ache settles in, and I have
a final layer of summer sun to roll across

my bedroom walls come tomorrow—
this bugle-call hue like a bottle of snake oil
promising zip and zing, up and at 'em,
pep in my step and starch in my collar.

Valerie Nieman

I open the blinds

Crows fly.

Everyone's hand
is against them
but I love them,

they'll eat
anything.

Valerie Nieman

Home

I don't know how long
it will last, this sagging
board fence that I've propped
with rebar and screwed to posts
loose in their sockets.

I should have ripped
the whole thing out, but
couldn't obliterate a village
of lichen that might
live for decades yet.

Myself, I'm borrowing
against time
I do not own, putting
muscle and bone
into the retirement cottage,

hoping that like a clock
with an exceedingly intricate
movement, the house will unwind
tick by slow tock,
until, long after me, it is

again as I found it,
peeling and out of square,
shabby as an ancient
apple tree nearly
merged with the ground.

Jennifer Browne

Dharma

Admiring your deft hands
untangling bladderwrack
from rasped ribbon,
it's my own carelessness
I'm cursing, atoning all
the meaningless, empty
things discarded, harms
I've wrought and never
had to witness in places,
even, I've never been.
And this one I nearly left,
glinting wrack line mylar,
nearly gave up because
I couldn't snap the plastic,
wouldn't fit that sanded
clot of refuse in a pocket.
But you, patient one,
turned your tending
to unthreading, gave
the moment its moment
to fix this one small wrong.

Jennifer Browne

On Finding *Huckster* Listed as an Occupation in the 1870 Census

Nibbed cursive, it's named
among the farmers, cobblers.
I think of snakes, oil, patter.
Reading later, I'm brought
to tin peddlers sharpening
scissors, to neighbors hauling
cabbages in off-day wagons.
Another name for *huckster*
is *butter and eggs man*.
And, oh, is this what you are?
Clattering to town, your cart
heaped with sweet, churned
smoothness, calling
to attention all my eggs?

Jessica Cory

Lullaby in Lane Three

The bespectacled cashier scans my organic raspberries,
pork rinds, avocadoes, ranch dressing, her gray bob sways
slightly off-tempo to "What's Love Got To Do With It"
settling into the store from ceilinged speakers, reminding

her and many of us that the hits of our day, like us,
are no longer cool or in fashion. Opposed to this
tune, she hums instead of chatting about the incoming
storm. Her melody of mostly minor keys reminds me

of a lullaby my mother's father hummed to his mother-
less children, a slow short strain, swaying in his throat,
a song my mother recalled from his lips, sacred as a hymn
traveling at the speed of sound to my ears, sleepy

with the buzz of summer's cicadas and the floor fan's
steady pulse. Here, in checkout lane three, the beep
of my butter in the sure hand of Deb, her blue
nameplate reads, evokes blood memories bone deep.

Jessica Cory

Bad Track

Early mornings, pre-work or pre-church
or pre-Saturday errands, my mother spackled
her face with Cover Girl's Warm Beige, waved
her magic L'Oréal mascara wand in Deepest Brown
across her eyelids and repeated her regular incantation
into our apartment's only bathroom mirror:
Man, I look like five miles of bad track.

My dad used to fix tracks for the C&O
in the late '70s and early '80s. He had
long dark hair then, told me how his boss hated
hippies, how it was always ten degrees warmer
or colder next to all that steel depending on the season,
how he witnessed the gray brains of his foreman's son
spackle the cracks in the track when Junior didn't hear
the engine round the bend. Noises echo in those hills, after all.

They call scars from injecting substances into one's veins
track marks, as though it's possible to track someone's history
through the scars they leave behind. Or maybe these small speckles
dotting elbows and the absences between toes are more
akin to tracking an injured animal, following its bloody sprinklings
until you locate the vacant body. My ex used to walk
to the 84 lumber yard just across the train tracks
from our small apartment to visit his dealer, coming home
with a bun, enough baggies that he'd be able to lay down track
after track in the recording studio and play enough gigs to get more.

A few months back, a Norfolk Southern train fell off the tracks
in East Palestine without a way to trace the impact
of vinyl chloride, butyl acrylate, and isobutylene on the fish,
soil, people who called (and still call) that place home. But it wasn't
the track's fault; instead some faulty rotor or axel or computer
should have functioned properly but failed. There is no person
to blame, no one to call and ask if symptoms should be tracked,
if the water is safe to drink, if the garden can be planted this year.

Home is sacred. No one wants their homes
or lives derailed. We don't want folks
tracking in dirt or dirty laundry; we deserve
safe spaces to examine the islands in our riverine
veins, to utter incantations in our bathroom
mirrors, to sing along to Dylan's *Blood on the Tracks* off-key.

CONTRIBUTOR NOTES:

KB Ballentine loves to travel and practice sword fighting and Irish step dancing: those Scottish and Irish roots run deep! When not tucked in a corner reading or writing, she makes daily classroom appearances to her students. Learn more at www.kbballentine.com.

Jennifer Browne falls in love easily with other people's dogs. She likes a nap on a sun-warmed rock and any kind of foraging. A creature of liminal spaces, she secretly believes she's a selkie. Her chapbook, *whisper song*, is forthcoming from tiny wren publishing.

Sarah Diamond Burroway is an eastern Kentucky writer whose work is featured in *The Bitter Southerner, Women Speak* anthologies of the Women of Appalachia Project, and *Still: The Journal*, where her essay, "Touch," won Judge's Choice" for nonfiction (2017). She's a proud Appalachian native and works in nonprofit grants administration.

Catherine Carter's collections of poetry include *Larvae of the Nearest Stars, The Swamp Monster at Home, The Memory of Gills*, all with LSU Press, and *Marks of the Witch* (Jacar Press, 2014.) Her work has also appeared in *Best American Poetry 2009, Orion, Ecotone, Poetry*, and *Ploughshares,* among others.

Jessica Cory is a writer and scholar from southeastern Ohio now living and working in western North Carolina. She is the editor of *Mountains Piled upon Mountains: Appalachian Nature Writing in the Anthropocene* and the co-editor (with Laura Wright) *of Appalachian Ecocriticism and the Paradox of Place.*

As a kid growing up in Ironton, Ohio, **Omope Carter Daboiku** wanted to be a writer. Her first published short story was nominated for the Pushcart Prize. Her favorite style is memoir, but she has been known to knock out a poem when necessary. She now lives in Dayton.

Kathleen Driskell is an award-winning poet and teacher and author of five books including most recently *The Vine Temple*, from Carnegie Mellon University Press. Her poems and essays have appeared in *The New Yorker, Riverteeth, Appalachian Review, Shenandoah, Southern Review*, and *Rattle.* Kathleen is Chair of the Naslund-Mann Graduate School of Writing at Spalding University.

A native East Tennessean, **Sue Weaver Dunlap** lives deep in the Southern Appalachian Mountains near Walland, Tennessee. Her work has appeared in various journals. Her poetry books include *A Walk to the Spring House* (Iris Press, 2021), *Knead* (Main Street Rag, 2016), and *The Story Tender* (Finishing Line Press, 2014).

Ellis Elliott has a blended family of six grown sons and lives in Juno Beach, FL. She has an MFA from Queens University, is a contributing writer for the *Southern Review of Books and* facilitates online writing groups called *Bewilderness Writing.* Her first chapbook is titled *Break in the Field.*

Lynette Ford was born in Western Pennsylvania, in a small city of steel, rail and coal. A fourth-generation Affrilachian storyteller, Lyn cherishes the gifts of narrative from her family. Lyn's work as storyteller, writer and teaching artist has taken her to Australia, Ireland, and across the United States.

Connie Jordan Green lives on a hilltop farm in East Tennessee where she writes poetry, novels for young people, and, for over 42 years, a newspaper column. Her work has received numerous awards, including Pushcart nominations for the poetry. Although retired from full-time teaching, she frequently leads writing workshops.

Kari Gunter-Seymour is the Poet Laureate of Ohio. Her focus is on lifting up underrepresented voices and working with incarcerated teens and adults and women in recovery. Her current collection is titled *Dirt Songs* (EastOver Press 2024). Her poetry has been featured in many publications including *Verse Daily, World Literature Today*, *The New York Times* and *Poem-a-Day*. (www. karigunterseymourpoet.com)

Pauletta Hansel's ninth poetry collection *Heartbreak Tree* (Madville Publishing, 2022) won the Poetry Society of Virginia's North American Book Award. She was Writer-in-Residence for The Public Library of Cincinnati/Hamilton County and Cincinnati's first Poet Laureate. Publications include *Oxford American, Rattle, Pine Mountain Sand & Gravel,* and *Poetry Daily*. (https://paulettahansel. wordpress.com)

Melissa Helton is Literary Arts Director at Hindman Settlement School. Her work appears in *Shenandoah, Norwegian Writers Climate Campaign, Appalachian Review, Still: The Journal*, and more. Her chapbooks include *Inertia: A Study* (2016) and *Hewn* (2021). She is editor of the anthology *Troublesome Rising: A Thousand-Year Flood in Eastern Kentucky* (2024).

Sara Henning is the author of *View from True North* (Southern Illinois University Press, 2018) and *Terra Incognita* (Ohio University Press, 2022). Her forthcoming collection of poems, *Burn*, is a Crab Orchard Series in Poetry Editor's Selection. She is an assistant professor at Marshall University.

Mikelle Hickman-Romine is a poet and craft artist based in Columbus, Ohio. She was reared by the Ohio River watershed, sucks the nectar from red clover blossoms, and is an award-winning artist and poet. Her ancestors rest in Appalachia, the only hills older than bone.

East Tennessean **Jane Hicks** is an award-winning poet, teacher, and quilter. Her first book, *Blood and Bone Remember* won several awards. The University Press of Kentucky published her poetry book, *Driving with the Dead*, in the fall of 2014. It won the Appalachian Writers Association Poetry Book of the Year Award and was a finalist for the Weatherford Award. Her new book, *The Safety of Small Things* will debut in January of 2024 from the University Press of Kentucky under the Fireside Industries imprint.

Karen Paul Holmes has had a cabin in the North Georgia mountains for 20 years. Her poetry books are *No Such Thing as Distance* (Terrapin) and *Untying the Knot* (Aldrich). Poems have appeared on *The Writer's Almanac, The Slowdown, Verse Daily, Diode* and many more journals.

Keri Johnson is a poet and journalist from southeast Ohio. Johnson's work is inspired by the people, land and history of what we call Appalachia; as well as her own family's folkways. She is passionate about capturing the region's stories, whether it be through her poetry or the press.

Jennifer Schomburg Kanke lived in Athens County, Ohio for 17 years before moving to Florida. Her work has appeared in *New Ohio Review* and *Shenandoah*. She is a winner of the Sheila-Na-Gig Editor's Choice Award for Fiction. She serves as a reader for *The Dodge*.

Leatha Kendrick's poetry and prose appear in journals and anthologies, including *Tar River Poetry, Southern Poetry Review, New Madrid Review, The Southern Poetry Anthology, Volume 3* and *What Comes Down to Us – Twenty-Five Contemporary Kentucky Poets*. Her fifth poetry collection poetry is *And Luckier* (2020). She lives in Lexington, Kentucky.

Helga Kidder's poems have been published in *Orbis, Lit Shark, Bloodroot*, and others. She has five collections of poetry, *Wild Plums, Luckier than the Stars, Blackberry Winter, Loving the Dead* which won the Blue Light Press Book Award 2020, and *Learning Curve*, poems about immigration and assimilation.

Natalie Kimbell was born in Norton Virginia, but grew up in Sequatchie County, Tennessee. Her work appears in *Pine Mountain Sand and Gravel, Mildred Haun Review, Anthology of Appalachian Writers: Kingsolver Edition, Tennessee Voices*, and *Artemis*. Her chapbook, *On Phillips Creek*, will be published by Finishing Line Press in 2024.

Patsy Kisner's poems have most recently appeared in *Still: The Journal, Appalachian Journal, Pine Mountain Sand & Gravel*, and *Women Speak*. She is the author of a poetry chapbook, *Inside the Horse's Eye*, and a poetry collection, *Last Days of an Old Dog*, both released from Finishing Line Press.

Originally from Virginia, **Lisa Kwong** is AppalAsian, an Affrilachian Poet, and author of *Becoming AppalAsian* (Glass Lyre Press). Her poems have appeared in *Best New Poets, A Literary Field Guide to Southern Appalachia, Anthology of Appalachian Writers*, and other publications. She teaches at Indiana University and Ivy Tech Community College.

Dawn Leas is the author *A Person Worth Knowing, Take Something When You*, and *I Know When to Keep Quiet*. Her poetry has appeared in *Verse-Virtual, New York Quarterly, The Paterson Literary Review, Literary Mama, The Pedestal Magazine, SWWIM*, and elsewhere. She's a writing coach, manuscript consultant, and arts educator.

Cathy Cultice Lentes has lived in the Appalachian foothills of southeast Ohio for over 35 years. She is the author of *Getting the Mail* (Finishing Line Press) and coauthor of *Stronger When We Touch* (The Orchard Street Press). Cathy holds a writing degree from the Solstice MFA Program near Boston.

Meagan Lucas is the award-winning author of *Songbirds and Stray Dogs* and *Here in the Dark: Stories*. She teaches Creative Writing at Robert Morris University, and in the Great Smokies Writing Program at UNCA. She is the Editor-in-Chief of *Reckon Review*. Meagan lives in the mountains of Western North Carolina.

Jessica Manack holds degrees from Hollins University and lives with her family in Pittsburgh, Pennsylvania. Her work has appeared widely in literary journals and anthologies. She is a recipient of a 2022 Curious Creators Grant and is finishing her first collection of poetry. Learn more at (http://www.jessicamanack.com).

Karen Salyer McElmurray's essays have won numerous awards, among them the Annie Dillard Prize, the Orison Anthology Award and the LitSouth Award. A collection of essays called *Voice Lessons* was released by Iris Books in 2020. A new collection called *I Could Name God in Twelve Ways* is forthcoming with University Press of Kentucky.

Wendy McVicker served as Poet Laureate of Athens, Ohio from 2020 to 2022. Her most recent chapbook is *Zero, a Door* (The Orchard Street Press, 2021). Her collaborative collection with poet Cathy Cultice Lentes, *Stronger When We Touch*, is from The Orchard Street Press.

Barbara Marie Minney, a seventh generation Appalachian, is an award-winning poet, teaching artist, and quiet activist. Barbara is the author of *If There's No Heaven*, the *Poetic Memoir Chapbook Challenge*, and *Dance Naked With God*. Barbara lives in Tallmadge, Ohio, with her wife of 42 years. Follow Barbara at (www.barbaramarieminneypoetry.com).

Laura Leigh Morris is the author of *The Stone Catchers* (UP Kentucky, forthcoming) and *Jaws of Life* (West Virginia UP, 2018). She teaches creative writing and literature at Furman University in Greenville, SC.

V.C. Myers is the author of *Ophelia* (Femme Salvé Books, 2023) and *Give the Bard a Tetanus Shot* (Vegetarian Alcoholic Press, 2019). Her work appears in journals such as *EPOCH, Poet Lore, Prairie Schooner, Still, Spillway, Appalachian Heritage,* and *Appalachian Journal*. An Appalachian poet, she lives in West Virginia.

Karen Whittington Nelson writes poetry and fiction from her Southeast Ohio farm. Her work is published in *Women Speak, Sheila-Na-Gig Online, Main Street Rag, Gyroscope Review, Pine Mountain Sand & Gravel, Anthology of Appalachian Writers, Northern Appalachia Review,* and *I Thought I Heard a Cardinal Sing: Ohio's Appalachian Voices*.

Valerie Nieman is the author of *In the Lonely Backwater* (2022 Sir Walter Raleigh Award), four earlier novels, and three books of poetry, *Leopard Lady: A Life in Verse* the most recent. A graduate of West Virginia University and Queens University of Charlotte, she has held state and NEA fellowships.

Elaine Fowler Palencia grew up in Morehead, KY, and Cookeville, TN. She has authored two collections of Appalachian short stories, four poetry chapbooks, and a work of Civil War history about her great-great grandfather of Appalachian Georgia. She reviews poetry books for *Pegasus*, journal of the Kentucky State Poetry Society.

Lisa J. Parker is a native Virginian, a poet, musician, and photographer. Her first book, *This Gone Place,* won the 2010 Weatherford Award, her second book, *The Parting Glass,* won the 2021 Arthur Smith Poetry Prize, and she is widely published in literary journals. Her work may be found at (www.wheatpark.com).

Tina Parker is the author of three books of poetry, most recently *Lock Her Up* published by Accents Publishing in 2021. Tina grew up in Bristol, VA, and she is a long-time Kentucky resident. To learn more about her work, visit (www.tina-parker.org) or follow her on Instagram @tetched_poet.

Poet, playwright, essayist, and editor, **Linda Parsons** is the poetry editor for Madville Publishing and the copy editor for *Chapter 16,* the literary website of Humanities Tennessee. She is published in such journals as *The Georgia Review*, *Iowa Review*, *Prairie Schooner*, *Southern Poetry Review*, *Terrain*, *The Chattahoochee Review*, *Baltimore Review*, *Shenandoah*, and *American Life in Poetry*. Her sixth collection, with poetry and prose, is *Valediction*. Five of her plays have been produced by Flying Anvil Theatre in Knoxville, Tennessee.

Rhonda Pettit recently completed a manuscript of poems, *Burden of the Song*, that uses lyric, narrative, interrogative, and documentary forms to explore the relationship between her paternal white ancestors and slavery in Pendleton County, Kentucky. She is a professor of English at the University of Cincinnati Blue Ash College.

Sara Pisak is a reviewer, essayist, and poet. Sara recently published work in *The Rumpus, Hippocampus, the Deaf Poets Society, Door = Jar, Poetry in Transit*, and *Appalachian Journal*, among others. In total, she published over 100 pieces. When not writing, Sara spends time with her family and friends.

Cat Pleska, award-winning author, educator, president of Mountain State Press, and 7th generation Appalachian, holds an MFA in creative nonfiction writing. Her memoir, *Riding on Comets* was published by West Virginia University Press, 2015. Her essays have appeared in *Still: The Journal, Heartwood Magazine, Change 7 Magazine*, and many others.

Bonnie Proudfoot's fiction, poetry, reviews, and essays have appeared in journals and anthologies. Her novel, *Goshen Road*, received the 2022 WCONA Book of the Year Award and was long-listed for the 2021 PEN/ Hemingway Award. Her poetry chapbook, *Household Gods*, was published in 2022 by Sheila-Na-Gig. She lives in Athens, Ohio.

Rita Quillen's most recent poetry book, *Some Notes You Hold* (Madville 2020) received a Bronze Medal from the Feathered Quill Book Awards, a finalist listing for poetry in the American Writing Awards, and is a Bonus Book for the 2023 International Pulpwood Queens and Timber Guys Book Club. Her novel, *Wayland*, published by Iris Press in 2019, was the March 2022 Bonus Book of the Month for the International Pulpwood Queens and Timber Kings Book Club. It is a sequel to her first novel, *Hiding Ezra* (Little Creek Books, 2014).

Suzanne S. Rancourt, is of Abenaki/Huron, Quebecois, Scottish descent, a USMC/Army Veteran, the winner of NU Press & Native Writers' Circle of the Americas First Book Award for *Billboard in the Clouds*, the Poetry of Modern Conflict Award for *murmurs at the gate*, author of *Old Stones, New Roads*, MSR Pub and *Songs of Archilochus*, Unsolicited Press, autumn 2023.

Erin Miller Reid is a physician and writer in Kingsport, Tennessee. Her work has appeared in *Still: The Journal, Appalachian Review, North Carolina Literary Review, Pine Mountain Sand and Gravel, The Women of Appalachia Project Anthology,* and the forthcoming anthology, *Troublesome Rising: A Thousand-Year Flood in Eastern Kentucky.*

Barbara Sabol hales from the hogbacks of western Pennsylvania, a place that shapes her poetry and values. Her book, *WATERMARK: Poems of the Johnstown Flood of 1889*, is from Alternating Currents Press. Her honors include an Individual Excellence Award from the Ohio Arts Council. Barbara lives in Akron, Ohio.

Shei Sanchez writes from her farm in Stewart, Ohio. Her work appears in many places, most recently *Sheila-Na-Gig online, Women Speak*, the Cuyahoga Valley National Park project with the Wick Center, and *Les Delices Music Meditations*. A Best of the Net nominee, Shei thanks her goats for keeping her sane.

Susan Truxell Sauter's work is published in *Voices from the Attic, Women Speak, Dionne's Story, Nasty Women & Bad Hombres*, and elsewhere. In 2023, part of her poem *Academy Awards of Expendable*, published 2016 in a national Fracture anthology, had its world premiere in Toronto as a song.

Leigh Claire Schmidli writes essays and fiction, enjoys reading work with lyrical leanings, and cooks elaborate meals that remind her of home. She'll use onions in just about anything, even a story. Her writing has been honored by A Room of Her Own Foundation and the Kentucky Foundation for Women.

Roberta Schultz, author of four chapbooks and one full-length collection of poetry, is a songwriter, teacher, and poet from Wilder, KY. She writes some of her songs on a mountain in North Carolina. She is co-founder of the *Poet & Song House Concert Series* with her Raison D'Etre trio mates.

Sharon Shadrick is a writer from Dunlap, Tennessee. She holds a bachelor's degree in Middle Grades Education and taught for eighteen years, retiring in 2022. Her work-in-progress is a nonfiction book, *The Power of a Paper Clip*. She enjoys morning coffee and writing with her 6 AM group, Rules Schmoolz.

Rose Smith appears in *The Examined Life, Pirene's Fountain, Snapdragon, Blood and Thunder, Minola Review,* and others. She is author of four chapbooks, including *Holes in My Teeth* (Kattywompus Press, 2016). Her collection, *Unearthing Ida,* won the 2018 Lyrebird Prize from Glass Lyre Press. She is a Cave Canem Fellow.

Lacy Snapp is a poet and woodworker in East Tennessee. She received her MFA from VCFA in 2023. Her first chapbook, *Shadows on Wood,* was published in 2021 by Finishing Line Press. She currently teaches at ETSU, runs her business, Luna's Woodcraft, and serves on the board of the Johnson City Poets Collective and as the Assistant Director of the Bert C. Bach Written Word Initiative.

Natalie Sypolt lives and writes in West Virginia. She is the author of *The Sound of Holding Your Breath* and her work has appeared in *Glimmer Train, Appalachian Review*, and *Still*. She is co-editor of *Change Seven Magazine* and is a past president of the Appalachian Studies Association.

Jessica D. Thompson's poetry has appeared in journals such as *Appalachian Heritage, Atlanta Review, ONE ART*, and the *Southern Review*. Her poetry collection, *Daybreak and Deep* (Kelsay Books, 2022) was named a finalist in the American Book Fest Best Books of 2022 for Narrative Poetry. She lives in Southern Indiana.

Patricia Thrushart writes poetry and historical nonfiction. Her fourth book of poems, *Inspired by Their Voices: Poems from Underground Railroad Testimonies*, was published by Mammoth Books. She is co-editor of the blog *North/South Appalachia* and co-founder of the group Poets Against Racism USA.

Rebecca Titchner is a resident of Ridgway, PA, on the edge of the Allegheny National Forest. For 24 years she has been the director of recycling programs in her county, Elk, and before that she spent a dozen years writing for two local daily newspapers.

E. J. Wade is a humanities educator and two-time Pushcart Award Nominee. She is published in the *Anthology of Appalachian Writers* and *The New Ohio Review*. Wade is pursuing a doctorate in Disability and Equity in Education at National Louis University and holds a Masters of Appalachian Studies from Shepherd University.

Jayne Moore Waldrop is the author of *Drowned Town*, named a 2022 Great Group Reads selection by the Women's National Book Association; *A Journey in Color: The Art of Ellis Wilson*; *Pandemic Lent: A Season in Poems,* and *Retracing My Steps*, a finalist in the New Women's Voices Chapbook Contest.

Kristi Stephens Walker is a writer and editor whose work has appeared in various print and online publications. A native of Charleston, WV, she currently lives in Nashville, TN where she has completed her first novel. She recently began work on an MFA at the Sewanee School of Letters.

Randi Ward is a poet, translator, lyricist, and photographer from Belleville, WV. She earned her MA in Cultural Studies from the University of the Faroe Islands and is a two-time recipient of the American-Scandinavian Foundation's Nadia Christensen Prize. Ward's work has been featured on *Folk Radio UK, NPR*, and *PBS NewsHour*. randiward.com/about

Kory Wells is the author of *Sugar Fix*, poetry from Terrapin Books. Her writing has been featured on *The Slowdown* from American Public Media and in many publications. A former poet laureate of Murfreesboro, Tennessee, she nurtures creative culture through arts advocacy, storytelling, and the from-home mentorship program MTSU Write.

Dana Wildsmith is the author of *With Access to Tools* and six previous collections of poetry, a novel, *Jumping,* and an environmental memoir, *Back to Abnormal: Surviving with an Old Farm in the New South*. Wildsmith has served as Artist-in-Residence for Grand Canyon National Park and Everglades National Park.

Athens, OH is home to **Kristine Williams** who came in 1985 to finish a master's degree and fell in love with the hills (and a boy). She is the author of *Like an Empty House* (Finishing Line Press) and has been involved with *Women Speak* since the beginning.

Meredith Sue Willis grew up in Shinnston, West Virginia. A writer-in-the-schools and professor of novel writing at New York University/SPS, she has published 24 books including fiction, children's novels, and nonfiction. She was an honoree of the Appalachian Literary Festival of Emory & Henry College. Learn more at meredithsuewillis.com.

Marianne Worthington is author of *The Girl Singer: Poems* (Univ. Press of KY, 2021), winner of the 2022 Weatherford Award for Poetry. She is co-founder and poetry editor of *Still: The Journal*, an online literary magazine. She grew up in Knoxville, Tennessee and lives, writes, and teaches in southeast Kentucky.

Karen Spears Zacharias is author of the forthcoming novel *No Perfect Mothers (Mercer University Press, Spring 2024)*. A daughter of Appalachia, Karen is a Weatherford Award Recipient for her novel *Mother of Rain*. Her work has been featured in the *New York Times, Washington Post, National Public Radio,* and in numerous anthologies.

ACKNOWLEDGMENTS:

Anthology of Appalachian Writers: "Tucking into the Backcountry,""Revival of the Fittest"

Appalachian Places: "What Bees Say"

Balance of Five: "For My Mountain Uncles, Those Men Long Gone," "One Thanksgiving I Made a General Jackson Pie"

Black Moon Magazine: "Three Times I Addressed the Moon as Jesus"

Blue Etiquette: Poems, Red Hen 2016: "Mowing the Fairways," and "What the Girl Wore"

Chautauqua Journal: "Driving Behind Rose in North Carolina"

Evening Street Review: "Peculiar"

Give the Bard a Tetanus Shot, Vegetarian Alcoholic Press: "The Stone Age"

Holes in My Teeth, Kattywompus Press: "First Bike"

New Ohio Review: "Our Grandmother"

OPEN: Journal of Arts and Letters: "Appalachian Triolet"

Shenandoah: "What the Girl Wore"

Still: The Journal: "On Cleaving"

The Tennessee Magazine: "Tradition Is a Body"

Valediction, Madville Publishing: "Come Home," "Light Around Trees in Morning," and "Visitation: Mother"

Will There be Singing, Shadeland Modern Press: "For the Friend Who Asked Me to Write a Poem About Breonna Taylor, 9/23/2020," "Com/passion," and "Dis/traction"

Sheila-Na-Gig Editions

9 781962 405423